A new musical based on
the novel by Miles Franklin

MY BRILLIANT CAREER

Book by **Sheridan Harbridge & Dean Bryant**
Music by Mathew Frank
Lyrics by Dean Bryant

CURRENCY PRESS
The performing arts publisher

MELBOURNE THEATRE COMPANY

CURRENT THEATRE SERIES

First published in 2024.
by Currency Press Pty Ltd,
Gadigal Land, Suite 310, 46–56 Kippax Street, Surry Hills, NSW 2010, Australia
enquiries@currency.com.au
www.currency.com.au

in association with Melbourne Theatre Company

Typeset by Brighton Gray for Currency Press..
Cover image shows Kala Gare; photo by Jo Duck.
Cover design by Sarah Ridgway-Cross.

Currency Press acknowledges the Traditional Owners of the Country on which we live and work. We pay our respects to all Aboriginal and Torres Strait Islander Elders, past and present.

A catalogue record for this book is available from the National Library of Australia

SHERIDAN HARBRIDGE is an award-winning actor, writer and director, graduating from NIDA in 2006. Her first musical *Songs for the Fallen* won Best Musical at the New York Music Theatre Festival in 2015, and a Green Room Award for Best Artist, appearing at Sydney, Brisbane and Auckland International Festivals, and Arts Centre Melbourne. In 2022 she directed *44 Sex Acts in One Week* for Sydney Festival, and the new Australian musical *Dubbo Championship Wrestling* for the Hayes Theatre, earning a best director nomination at the Sydney Theatre Awards. As a member of the Griffin Studio 2016, she developed and directed *Nosferatutu,* touring Griffin Theatre Company, Glenn Street and Adelaide Festival. As an actor she has appeared in *Meet Me at Dawn*, *Prima Facie*, *The Beast*, *The Speechmaker*, *North by Northwest* (Melbourne Theatre Company); *A Streetcar Named Desire, Stop Girl, Calamity Jane, The Sugar House, Girl Asleep, The Dog/The Cat* (Belvoir); *Kill Climate Deniers, Jump for Jordan* (Griffin Theatre Company); *Queen Fatima* (Sydney Festival); *Muriel's Wedding* (Sydney Theatre Company) and *Gaybies* (Darlinghurst). Recent TV credits include *The Twelve* (Foxtel) and *The Messenger* (ABC). Sheridan won Best Actress at the Sydney Theatre Awards for her performance in *Prima Facie*, and for Blanche DuBois in *A Streetcar Named Desire*.

DEAN BRYANT is an award-winning writer and director who was Associate Director of Melbourne Theatre Company (2016-2019), most recently directing *Bloom* for the Company. He met partner Mathew Frank while studying at WAAPA where they wrote *Prodigal*, which won the Green Room Award and was produced off-Broadway. Other musicals include *Once We Lived Here* (Green Room award), *Virgins: A Musical Threesome, The Silver Donkey* and songs for *Mr & Mrs Murder.* Dean created verbatim theatre plays *Gaybies* and *Well...that Happened.* Cabaret work includes Christie Whelan-Browne vehicles *Show People* and *Britney Spears: The Cabaret*. He wrote and directed the short *Rhyme Time*. Recent credits as director include *Dear Evan Hansen* (Sydney Theatre Company/Michael Cassel Group), *La Boheme* (Opera Australia), *Candide* (Victorian Opera), *A Little Night Music* (Hayes Theatre, Sydney Theatre

award); *Giustino* (Pinchgut); *Fun Home* (Melbourne Theatre Company/ Sydney Theatre Company, Sydney Theatre, Green Room Awards); *Hubris & Humiliation* (Sydney Theatre Company) and *The Normal Heart* (STCSA). Other Melbourne Theatre Company credits include *Torch the Place*, *Kiss of the Spider Woman*, *Lady in the Van*, *An Ideal Husband*, *Wild*, *Vivid White*, *Born Yesterday*, *Skylight*, *I'll Eat You Last* and *Next to Normal*.

MATHEW FRANK is an award-winning composer, sound designer and music director who has worked on numerous Melbourne Theatre Company productions including *Fun Home*, *Lady in the Van*, *An Ideal Husband*, *Skylight*, *Private Lives*, *The Drowsy Chaperone*, *Next to Normal*, *Well*, *That Happened* and for Sydney Theatre Company, *Hubris & Humiliation*. He met partner Dean Bryant at WAAPA and their first musical, *Prodigal*, won a Green Room Award and was produced off-Broadway. They followed this with *Once We Lived Here* (Green Room Award), *Virgins: A Musical Threesome*, *The Silver Donkey* and the songs for *Mr & Mrs Murder*. He composed the score for short *Rhyme Time* and created Christie Whelan-Browne vehicles *Show People* and *Britney Spears: The Cabaret*. Other credits as music director include *A Funny Thing Happened on the Way to the Forum* (Gordon Frost Organisation); *Jerry's Girls*, *La Cage Aux Folles* and *Pirates of Penzance* (The Production Company).

Contents

Director Anne-Louise Sarks and Choreographer Amy Campbell in rehearsal (Photo: Charlie Kinross)

Director Anne-Louise Sarks in rehearsal (Photo: Charlie Kinross)

A Conversation with the Authors

Dean Bryant, Sheridan Harbridge and Mathew Frank

Why did you want to adapt My Brilliant Career?

DB: We all grew up in rural areas—Sheridan and I, like Sybylla, on dairy farms—and loved that the story was about a young person who didn't fit in and was searching for their place in the world, for some way to live a creative life.

SH: I was really excited to take on such an iconic book that every generation has grown up with. Every time I would tell people we were adapting it, just the absolute emotions that would pour out of them about how much they loved that book growing up... It was really exciting to take on and bring their version of Sybylla to life.

What was behind the decision to turn it into a musical?

DB: It felt like a story that would enlarge by being sung. We had the idea of a teenage girl in her room writing out her angst in piano ballads. The score has always lived in that world, and we needed to tune the script to match the energy we were aiming for.

MF: Working with actor-musicians is the most exciting thing to see, it's like Olympic athletes. Getting the orchestra out of the pit and onstage, being musician, singer and actor—it's a thrilling thing not to separate the disciplines.

DB: The novel is epic, with Sybylla spinning from place to place and her mood changing constantly. We wanted to capture that dynamism in the musical. The way she talks to the reader immediately opened up a way for her to talk to the audience. This became even more exciting when we transformed the show into an actor-musician version, reimagining her as the front girl of a band, taking us into almost a gig version of her life.

MF: Musically, I loved the idea of someone finding their voice, so I could use my own composer's voice while marrying that to modern music, working in different pop genres—like a Sybylla mixtape—but also playing with folk songs and music of the day. So there's my voice as a composer, my pastiche of pop/rock, alongside a pastiche of music from the time.

SH: Can I add to that I think those three phases are interesting, because we take on the three phases of feminism: her era, feminism from the seventies when the book was republished and had that huge cultural place with the film and then the feminism of now, which is a different cultural beast.

How does Sybylla's story intersect with where feminism is now?

SH: The current phase of feminism is very close to the inner world of Sybylla in 1896, which was contradictory. She wasn't trying to be a perfect, ideal, strong woman; she's gloriously selfish and lets herself go down any path and follow any impulse without censoring it. I think there have been phases with feminism when women have had to be flawless, to be a wall of strength but now we're embracing imperfection—that's true equality. What's exciting about adapting the book is that it was successful, not just for feminism in the moment, which was not spoken about much, but also because it was distinctly Australian and that was what was so unique: an Australian feminist story. We crave to hear our own voice on stage and it's fun to incorporate what Australia is now into the work.

What was the writing process like?

DB: Mathew and I have collaborated as co-writers for a quarter of a century now, so we were used to the joys and struggles that come from that. But bringing a co-writer onto the script was exciting and scary. Sheridan and I have now worked in so many different modes, and what's really rewarding is that you can keep taking the reins as one of you feels strongly about what needs to happen next. When you trust the person there's a massive sense of relief in sharing the load.

At its heart, what do you think this version of My Brilliant Career *is about?*

SH: The story is about a young artist striving to find a mode of expression. We are all here because of the risk that Miles Franklin took at a terrifying time to be an artist and make her way in the world. I am here because of this, and to see the offspring of that risk in full flight in their form of art is the perfect journey for this work. It's about how Sybylla, as an artist, is someone who exists outside the matrix but pushes back against the structure women are placed in that doesn't make sense. That is a timeless story, questioning why we build societies as they are. It's ultimately about joy and rebellion–

MF: —about taking a risk to share what the world might not want to hear—

DB: —and how the place you wanted to escape from feeds what you ultimately create.

Writer (book) Sheridan Harbridge and Assistant Director Miranda Middleton in rehearsal (Photo: Charlie Kinross)

Drew Livingston in rehearsal (Photo: Charlie Kinross)

Kala Gare and Raj Labade in rehearsal (Photo: Charlie Kinross)

My Brilliant Career was first performed by Melbourne Theatre Company at Southbank Theatre, The Sumner, Melbourne, on the lands of the Boon Wurrung and Wurundjeri peoples of the Kulin Nation, on 7 November 2024 with the following cast and creatives:

FRANK / ENSEMBLE	Cameron Bajraktarevic-Hayward
JIMMY / HORACE / ENSEMBLE	Lincoln Elliott
ENSEMBLE	Victoria Falconer
SYBYLLA MELVYN	Kala Gare
HARRY / PETER / ENSEMBLE	Raj Labade
FATHER / JAY-JAY / M'SWAT / ENSEMBLE	Drew Livingston
GERTIE / BLANCHE / ENSEMBLE	HaNy Lee
GRANNIE / ROSE JANE / ENSEMBLE	Ana Mitsikas
MOTHER / HELEN / MRS M'SWAT / ENSEMBLE	Christina O'Neill
ENSEMBLE	Jarrad Payne

Book, Sheridan Harbridge
Book & Lyrics, Dean Bryant
Music, Mathew Frank
Director, Anne-Louise Sarks
Musical Director, Victoria Falconer
Choreographer, Amy Campbell
Set & Costume Designer, Marg Horwell
Lighting Designer, Matt Scott
Orchestrator / Vocal Arranger, James Simpson
Sound Designer, Joy Weng
Assistant Director, Miranda Middleton
Assistant Musical Director, Drew Livingston
Assistant Set & Costume Designer, Savanna Wegman

Kala Gare in rehearsal (Photo: Charlie Kinross)

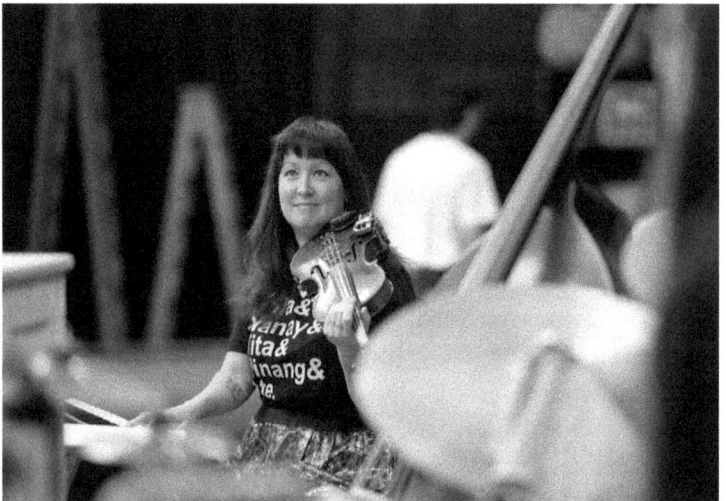

Musical Director Victoria Falconer in rehearsal (Photo: Charlie Kinross)

To my dear Indyana. This story is all about you.
For no other purpose do I tell it.
Love, Sheridan x

Indyana Hopman
5 March 2004 ~ 22 March 2024

Musical Director Victoria Falconer, Drew Livingston, Ana Mitsikas, Kala Gare, Lincoln Elliott, Christina O'Neill, HaNy Lee and Cameron Bajraktarevic-Hayward in rehearsal (Photo: Charlie Kinross)

Musical Director Victoria Falconer, Drew Livingston, Raj Labade, Ana Mitsikas, Lincoln Elliott, Kala Gare, Jarrad Payne, HaNy Lee, Christina O'Neill and Cameron Bajraktarevic-Hayward in rehearsal (Photo: Charlie Kinross)

CHARACTERS

SYBYLLA
LUCY
DICK
HORACE
GERTIE
GRANNIE
DRIVER
FRANK
HELEN
JAY JAY
HARRY
BLANCHE
JIMMY
M'SWAT
MRS M
LIZER
ROSE-JANE
BULLANT
PETER

NOTES

My Brilliant Career is written for a cast of ten actor-musicians, the Balladeers. Eight play all the roles, with two dedicated musicians. The character doubling is as follows:

SYBYLLA
HARRY/PETER
LUCY/HELEN/MRS M
DICK/JAY-JAY/M'SWAT
FRANK/BULLANT
HORACE/JIMMY
GERTIE/BLANCHE/LIZER
GRANNIE/ROSE-JANE

Dialogue in bold indicates direct address by Sybylla.

Melbourne Theatre Company acknowledges the Boon Wurrung and Wurundjeri Woi Wurrung peoples of the Kulin Nation, the traditional custodians of the land on which we work, create and gather. We pay our respects to all First Nations people, their Elders past and present, and their enduring connections to Country, knowledge, and stories. As a Company we remain committed to the invitation of the Uluru Statement from the Heart and its call for voice, truth and treaty.

This play text went to press before the end of rehearsals and may differ from the play as performed.

ACT ONE

A dry Australian field. A beaten upright piano grows out of the hardy, resilient grass. A group of musicians, the BALLADEERS, *are warming up for a gig—chatting, plugging in instruments, coming and going, trying music out—what the punters see anytime they turn up to a pub gig or music festival.* SYBYLLA *enters and pulls out a microphone.*

SYBYLLA: **My dear fellow Australians**
Just a few quick words to tell you
That this story
Is going to be all about
Me.
For no other purpose do I tell it. I make no apologies for being egotistical. Because I am.

The BALLADEER *who'll play* HARRY *begins to play the the Prologue on the guitar. He's hot.* SYBYLLA *admonishes us:*

This is not a romance!
I am far too clever to be some silly heroine in some silly romance.
There is no plot to this story. I am from a class of individuals not given time for a plot.

The female BALLADEERS *pick up the Prologue.*

Like my sisters of toil on this sun cracked horizon, the scrubbing of pots, the squeezing of cows' teats and the ironing of doilies, is my God. given. plot.
SIDENOTE: Why must we iron doilies?!
But as pointless and as ineffective as my life may be, I have always dreamed … no … I have always known, that I belonged to the world of MORE.

The final four BALLADEERS *join and they all play together for the first time.* SYBYLLA *stops to revel in her creativity, demonstrated by the* BALLADEERS.

HELL YEAH! Eat your heart out Banjo Paterson!

NB: A note on the BALLADEERS—*they are* SYBYLLA*'s backing band, part of her, on her side, doing whatever she needs them to do—act parts, support her, help her work out her thoughts.*

It is 1899 and I regret to inform you that nothing happens. Nothing ever happens to poor girls like me. This is simply a yarn. A really real yarn.

I promise I won't talk too much.

I take that back. I am going to talk heaps. Suck it.

My dear fellow Australians. This is the story of My Brilliant, (question mark?) Career!

She leads the BALLADEERS *into a glorious crescendo to the Prologue. Then:*

SYBYLLA *steps forward, leaving the* BALLADEERS*. The sun blinds her.*

Once upon a time when the days were long and hot; I, Sybylla Melvyn, was fifteen years old and standing in a paddock, having my daily fight with God.

[*Calling up to God*] Is this what life is? Are you joking?? Are you even there?

My mother calls for me.

We hear LUCY *calling from the* BALLADEERS*.*

LUCY: Sybylla?

SYBYLLA: **I ignore her.**

LUCY: I know you're ignoring me!

SYBYLLA: **Lucy Bossier of Caddagat, the wealthy daughter of a squatter.**

LUCY: Where are you!?

SYBYLLA: **Edyyyucated and rrrrefined—**

SYBYLLA *connects with a* BALLADEER *who plays* LUCY.

LUCY: [*like a fishmonger's wife*] There you are, you useless girl!

SYBYLLA: **But then, she met my father.**

A BALLADEER *plays* DICK.

DICK: Answer your bloody mother when she calls for you, ya mongrel girl.

SYBYLLA: **Dick Melvyn, a man whose career ended when he brought us to Possum Gully, our barren farm of dry crooked scrub.**

DICK: Where's the rest of the useless lot?

SYBYLLA: **I despised him with the relentlessness of fifteen. That's a lot.**

LUCY: Horace! Gertie! The cow's down!

SYBYLLA: **My little brother Horace, all churlish resentment.**

HORACE: This sucks.

SYBYLLA: **His twin Gertie, all butterflies and tears.**

GERTIE: Poor moo cow!

BALLADEERS *play* HORACE *and* GERTIE.

We stare at our last cow, who's finally given in to the Great Drought. This does not look good.

They all stare out front as the cow moans.

GERTIE: Why won't the cow stand up?

HORACE: Are you dim? She's starving.

LUCY: Go fetch the Blackshaws—

SYBYLLA: **He won't fetch them. He's full of pride. And whisky.**

DICK: No! Get the ropes, Horace, we'll lift her up.

LUCY: If we don't get help, that beast is finished.

DICK: We don't need help.

SYBYLLA: We're way beyond help.

LUCY: Sybylla?

SYBYLLA: **Did I say that out loud?**

LUCY: Speak to your father with respect.

SYBYLLA: **I shouldn't, but I can't stop myself.**

Respect the man who bought a dairy in the middle of a drought?

LUCY: Hush your mouth.

SYBYLLA: Respect the man who brought us to the ass end of the earth so he could be king of something??

LUCY: Don't be vulgar!

SYBYLLA: King of the pub, he is.

DICK: Shut up shut up shut up! This is the hand we've been dealt!

SYBYLLA: This is the hand you dealt us!
And this, my dear fellow Australians, is life.

The BALLADEERS *kick in.* SYBYLLA *grabs a microphone and sings to us in fury.*

Song: 'LIFE AS WE KNOW IT'.

[*Singing*]
This. I mean what is this?
What are we doing this for, the three of us?
This. You brought us here for this?
The bright new life you dreamed for us—for you—is this?
This beast is stuck in the middle of the paddock
Can't even stand on her own four feet
And here we are in the middle of the paddock
What a stimulating, edifying, tasty treat
Come on Dad, just admit defeat!

I'll tell you what this is:
This is life as we know it
Life as we grow it
A life fed on dust and fear
And it chokes us
It's smoke and drought and I'm out!
I've had it up to here
Here
With my brilliant career
My b-b-b-b-b-b-b-b-b-b-brilliant career!

LUCY: How dare you talk to your father like that? You'll apologise to him.
SYBYLLA: **Of course she sticks up for him.**
LUCY: Do you think he enjoys seeing that beast in agony? You're a vicious thing, Sybylla. It's a wonder God doesn't strike you dead, the things that come out of that mouth.
SYBYLLA: **I briefly consider sharing my leanings towards atheism, but she's had a tough day.**
If there is a God he wouldn't torture me for his own amusement.
This grinding work every day, I hate it I hate it I hate it.
[*Singing*]

This, I'm not doing this
Going forwards with more of this—with you—
I mean it
This the place you bottomed out
Where plans became prison bars—this … piss!
This … this

You're both of you stuck in the middle of the paddock
Can't even stand on your own four feet
I'll murder you in the middle of this paddock
But you'll die before I do that, in this goddamn heat
Sweat it out, till we're dried-up meat

I'll tell you what I think
Of this life as we know it
Life as we blow it
Like the dust from our eyes and ears
It's enslaved us
I'll save myself from these chains
I've got to disappear
From here
And my brilliant career
My b-b-b-b-b-b-b-b-b-b-brilliant career!

A gunshot. They look at each other in panic.

Was that a gunshot?
LUCY: Dick!
SYBYLLA: …
LUCY: What's he done—
SYBYLLA: **Dad returns, bottle and rifle in hand.**
DICK: Shot the beast. Put her out of her misery.
SYBYLLA: **I'm relieved it's not him. I think.**
LUCY: Richard.
DICK: She wasn't going to make it. It's useless.
SYBYLLA: [*singing*]

We career from disaster to disaster
churning through them faster and faster
So dog-tired we barely despair

You've drunk away your dreams
And no-one cares it seems
She's sewing and praying
I'm going, not staying
But where where where where where??
To be free of what this is
Of this life as we know it
Life as you blow it
The ending is pretty clear
I'm awake now
I'll take the train from this time
Take it anywhere but here
Here
And a man full of ego and rum
And my magpie-screech of a mum
And my b-b-b-b-b-b-b-b-b-b-b-brilliant career!

That evening. The Melvyn children sit in a grim pall. SYBYLLA *plays on the out-of-tune piano, trying to make 'Wrong Key' work on the resistant keys.*

There were but two states of existence allotted to us poor—work and sleep. But I did a great amount of thinking between the two—for, PS, I'm afflicted with the power of thought (trust me, it's awful): 'why are there poor in this great country at all!' But I was starving for a third state of existence. Art and books and music … I was thirsty. A thirsty girl. Without art and music, it's highly possible my body could explode.

GERTIE: It's not father's fault it won't rain. Everyone's lost stock this summer.

HORACE: Not cos they got shot in the head, idiot.

GERTIE: Don't call me idiot, idiot.

HORACE *pinches* GERTIE.

GERTIE: Arrrrrch dooooornt Horace! Get off me?

HORACE: Make me.

SYBYLLA *sings, and though the piano is stubborn, the melody captivates the twins.*

This piano
Is tinny and out of tune
This piano
Is unpleasant to hear
This piano plays C-sharp, not C …
Like me
GERTIE: Did you write that?
HORACE: That's cool.

SYBYLLA *launches off the stool and grabs* HORACE *in a headlock.*
LUCY *has entered, unseen.*

SYBYLLA: Don't. Hurt. People. Smaller. Than. You.
HORACE: You're hurting *me* and I'm smaller than you!
SYBYLLA: **Here I teach Horace a lesson I learned long ago: life isn't fair.**
Stop hitting yourself stop hitting yourself stop hitting yourself.
HORACE: Doornt you dumb girl, I'll tell Mum.
LUCY: What will you tell me? That not one of you is in bed yet?

A terrible fright, GERTIE *cries and flees.*

Get to it! Where's your father?
HORACE: Where do you think?
LUCY: Take the buggy to the pub and fetch him. Sybylla, I want to talk to you.
SYBYLLA: **Conversation? In this house? Wowee thats new.**
LUCY: With the cattle gone, it's no use. We cannot afford to keep you at home.

SYBYLLA *stares at her mother.*

Do you think you could earn your own living?
SYBYLLA: Of course! I can! I want that more than anything.
LUCY: Good. I've found you a position as a governess.
SYBYLLA: What?! No!
LUCY: What do you mean no?
SYBYLLA: A governess! No, Mother, that would be torture!
LUCY: Oh the dramatics! You're too careless to be a nurse, your cooking's atrocious. You really are a very useless girl.
SYBYLLA: … There are other things I could do.

LUCY: Are there? Wonderful, pray tell me.

> SYBYLLA *pauses. She mumbles, no one can hear it.*

SYBYLLA: … Music.

LUCY: Beg pardon?

SYBYLLA: … music. I could play music. I could be a pianist.

LUCY: A pianist!?

SYBYLLA: I could be the Australian Mozart, for all we know!

LUCY: Well go on then—if you you're so good, walk out the door and show the world what a wonderful creature you are! Let's see how long you last out there on your own.

SYBYLLA: Mother, you are so cruel. Can't we ask Grannie Bossier to lend us money?

LUCY: I will not ask my mother for help.

SYBYLLA: I won't be a governess, I'm not doing it!

LUCY: Sybylla, I don't understand you at all.

SYBYLLA: I wish I was dead, so I could be born again as an idiot that would enjoy this life you seem to like.

LUCY: …

> You unfeeling girl. You must be mad, to say the things you do.

> LUCY *exits.* SYBYLLA *calls after her—*

SYBYLLA: I DO HAVE FEELINGS.

I am never in favour of hysterical leading ladies in stories— but oh HOW I HATED THIS LIVING DEATH THAT HAD SWALLOWED MY YOUTH AND SAPPED MY PRIME!

Gertie! I'm being overwhelmed by my hot untamed spirit!

GERTIE: Sybby, I'm sleeping.

SYBYLLA: Mother's right—I think I *am* mad. But what's the point of being alive if you're not living? Imagine we could be independent, Gertie. Go choose our own adventure.

GERTIE: I choose sleep.

SYBYLLA: I'd run away to the city to start a newspaper just to tell everyone this is friggin unfair. I wish we never left Caddagat. There were books, and people, and conversation—

GERTIE: And dancing—

SYBYLLA: Do you remember the balls?

GERTIE: Mother and Father would waltz all night.

Tell me one of your stories before we go to sleep.

SYBYLLA: No, I'm too tired and emotional.

GERTIE: Please?

SYBYLLA: Okay.

Song: 'PRINCE OF A GIRL'.

[*Singing*]

There was a magical land a million years ago
You've never seen a place so green it was botanic'lly 'whoa!'
The birds would sing, the ants wouldn't sting
And it was ruled by the handsomest and bravest king

DICK *appears, young and handsome.*

He'd stand on the verandah that he'd made from gum
Beside his queen, so damned serene she was basic'lly Mum

LUCY *enters, young, hopeful, lovely.*

They'd laugh and sing, never once arguing
As they gazed upon their treasure, their beloved offspring

SYBYLLA *plays as* DICK*'s beloved child again.*

And the king of the bush would lift up his heir
A child who was wild with a forest of hair
And whisper her fortune right into her ear
'Never fear, my girl—

BOTH: [*singing*]

—Never ever fear

DICK: [*singing*]

You can be anything, uh-oh uh-oh
You can rule the world
You can be anything, uh-oh uh-oh
My princess—no!—My prince of a girl'

SYBYLLA: [*singing*]

He had her riding a horse, before the girl could walk
He'd say

DICK: [*singing*]

'Debate this with my mate'—

SYBYLLA: [*singing*]
> When she could hardly even talk
> He'd often shout:

DICK: [*singing*]
> 'Go on, figure it out'

SYBYLLA: [*singing*]
> He cast a spell that dispelled her having a single doubt
> He'd stand on that verandah as his subjects fought
> To tell his queen, they should be seen in a much bigger court
> He'd laugh and smile, and after a while
> His kingdom felt too small and somehow cramped his style
> And the king of the bush lifted up his heir
> A child who'd been styled like the wild out there
> And whispered their fortune right into her ear

DICK: [*singing*]
> 'Never fear, my girl, never ever fear
> We can be anything, uh-oh uh-oh
> We can rule the world
> We can be anything, uh-oh uh-oh
> Your king and his prince of a girl'

> DICK *and* LUCY *age before our eyes and the bed becomes a cart.*

SYBYLLA: [*singing*]
> They left the magical land and found another place
> So brown and dry it baked your eyeballs into your face
> The birds would croak, the dust was like smoke
> And the king could not accept the royal bank was broke
> He'd stand on a verandah, made from rotten gum
> And try and think, but mainly drink, about how low they'd come
> The queen would shriek—

LUCY: [*singing*]
> 'You're so piss-weak'

SYBYLLA: [*singing*]
> While the rest of them would work until their bones'd creak
> And the king of the bush would stare at his heir
> A child who was wild with sudden despair
> And shouted their fortune for all to hear

DICK: [*singing*]
> 'This is fear, my girl, fear is here'
> Want to be anything, uh-oh uh-oh
> Want to rule the world?
> Want to be anything, uh-oh uh-oh
> Good luck, my prince of a girl
> Give in … girl
> Uh-oh, uh-oh

GERTIE: You're good at stories, Sybby. You should write them down.

SYBYLLA: Why?

GERTIE: For when I need them. Goodnight.

> GERTIE *sleeps.*

SYBYLLA: **And Gertie can just fall asleep. Wake up Gertie! Don't you know that everything is wrong in the world?? Women must follow their husbands into oblivion! A girl must have no ambition but to serve! The poor stay poor as the rich get richer—the wheels of social mechanism need readjusting! It's all upside-down!**

I wished I was more like Gertie, where a new dress and a picnic was the bestest day ever. Then I could finally sleep, absolutely sure that I was in the right place, and the right time, in the right body. God—did you put a boy's dreams in a girl's body? Nah, boys are dumb.

But why was it only men who could take the world by its ears and conquer their fate? God, if you even are there—how friggin DARE you! I'm going to turn your kingdom upside down!

> *The* BALLADEERS *play as* SYBYLLA *begins to write down her story. Next day.*

GERTIE: Sybylla, have you slept?

SYBYLLA: I'LL NEVER SLEEP AGAIN GERTIE. MY MIND IS FIRE. AND IT WAS ALL YOU, YOU LITTLE GENIUS GRONK. I'm writing a book!

GERTIE: Are you writing your book over the bible?! Sybylla!

SYBYLLA: I'm already going to hell. Besides, no-one actually reads this thing.

GERTIE: [*in a disturbing close whisper of heated musk*] I read it. There are naked people in the first chapter.

The BALLADEERS *react in surprise.*

SYBYLLA: … Gertie.

We hear heavy breathing through GERTIE*'s nose.*

GERTIE: What's the story about?

SYBYLLA: I'm warning you, it's probably really good.

GERTIE: A fairy story?

SYBYLLA: YA. A fairy story in the outback.

GERTIE: The Australian outback? I'm getting cultural cringe but I'll try and be open to it.

SYBYLLA *tears out the pages and puts in an envelope.*

SYBYLLA: I'm going to send it, Gertie. I'm going to send it to Sydney's most important leading publisher.

GERTIE: Whaaaaaaa??

SYBYLLA *hands the letter to* GERTIE*, who hands it to a* BALLADEER *and it's passed on.*

SYBYLLA: I might make money of my own, Gerts! I hear writers are all pretty much rich. **I could be a Lady Lawson! A Brontë of the Büsh, why not?**

The letter makes its way to HORACE *who leaves the* BALLADEERS *with it.*

HORACE: Sybyyyylla has a leee-tter.

SYBYLLA: Who from?

GERTIE: [*hyperventilating*] SYDNEY'S. MOST IMPORTANT. LEADING. PUBLISHER.

HORACE *won't give it to her, she tries to snatch it. He opens it and reads it.*

HORACE: To the author of *The Ivory Tower and the Talking Owl.*

He snorts.

Thank you for the submission of your unorthodox manuscript. It did improve some of the drier passages of Deuteronomy. The story showed great promise, but the writer's inexperience was too much in evidence for publication.

SYBYLLA: Inexperience?

HORACE: You can't write, you're just a stupid girl.

> SYBYLLA *grabs the letter, then his forearm. He squeals in anticipation of pain, but* SYBYLLA *doesn't twist his flesh.*

Arrrch Dooooorrrnt!

SYBYLLA: Yes, Horace. I *am* just a stupid girl. I don't have experience. I am experiencing all a girl will *ever* experience. But you? You could run away to the city, start a newspaper, write a symphony— be a pirate! While I stay here, sweeping the floors behind you, and when I die, my eulogy will be SO dull, it won't be published either. And history will never know I even existed.

> *She lets go of him.*

I'm off to experience ironing the doilies.

HORACE: … I'm frightened.

SYBYLLA: **Thus, my dear fellow Australians, life trundled on. I resigned myself to the fact that perhaps I was not as unique as I hoped, which KILLED me. I became so depressed I started to obey Mother—**

LUCY: Sybylla!

SYBYLLA: Yes, Mother?

LUCY: I know you're ignoring me—wait, what? Oh my goodness, I think Sybylla is ill!

SYBYLLA: **A fateful letter had arrived.**

> *A letter zips around* BALLADEERS, *ending with* GRANNIE.

LUCY: Grannie has written. About you.

> GRANNIE *leaves the* BALLADEERS.

SYBYLLA: **Grannie Bossier. She lives up to her surname … she's bossy.**

GRANNIE: 'Dearest Lucy, I am truly grieved to hear that Sybylla is such a source of grief to you. The girl must surely be ill or she would never act as you describe. She is young in regards to marriage, but it might be the makings of her if she married early—'

SYBYLLA: **Whoa … married!**

[*Reading out loud or along with* GRANNIE] ' … Gertie will be coming on soon, and Sybylla, being so very plain, will need all the time she can get.'

GRANNIE: 'This is an emergency. Send her up to me in Caddagat as soon as you can.'

SYBYLLA: Oh my God.

GERTIE: Sybylla …

SYBYLLA: Gertie …

GERTIE: Sybylla?

SYBYLLA: GERTIE.

GERTIE: You're going to Caddagat??

SYBYLLA: I'M PLAAAIN?

GERTIE: What?

SYBYLLA: GERTIE GRANNIE'S RIGHT I'M PLAIN.

LUCY: Lord save me.

SYBYLLA: I KNEW IT I'M PLAIN THIS IS A KNIFE IN MY HEART.

GERTIE: Sybby you're going to Caddagat?

SYBYLLA: IT'S MY NOSE, MY NOSE IT'S TOO SMALL OR TOO BIG I don't know it's too something—CADDAGAT WHAT OH YES CADDAGAT!! GERTIE I'M GOING TO CADDAGAT CADDAGAT CADDAGAT!!

They scream and scream and scream, HORACE *enters with* SYBYLLA's *bags and joins in the screaming, maybe the* BALLADEERS *start screaming, and we're off.*

DICK: You off, prince? Righto.

SYBYLLA: You're not taking me to the station?

DICK: [*exiting*] Gotta see a man about a dog.

SYBYLLA: What does that even mean?

LUCY: What are you wearing? Have you no interest in your appearance? Brush your hair at least!

SYBYLLA: Seeing as I'm so plaiiiiiinnnnn, I didn't see the point in trying.

LUCY: This is your chance, Sybylla. Caddagat is full of opportunity. If you won't work, you must marry. Be useful to someone at least.

LUCY *exits.*

GERTIE: You'll write us all the time?

SYBYLLA: No-one wants my writing, Gertie.

GERTIE: I do.

SYBYLLA: Well then … okay. I'll write you!

GERTIE: Honour bright?

SYBYLLA: Yes, really truly honour bright.

GERTIE: What will I do when Horace bullies me?

SYBYLLA: Do a wee in his boots, okay?

GERTIE: Okay.

SYBYLLA: Promise me you will always love me a little and never forget me.

They hug, nice and deep.

HORACE: You off to get married then?

SYBYLLA: No, I'm off to change the world!

HORACE: Who would marry you anyway, you never shut up.

SYBYLLA: [*whispering to* GERTIE] Go find his boots.

HORACE *joins the group hug.*

Ohhhhhhh I love you both.

Self-analysis! This is dull and sentimental. Best skip it.

She wipes her eyes, picks up her suitcase and walks, the Melvyns melt back into the BALLADEERS. *Thus begins her adventure.*

My dear fellow Australians! In particular, GIRLS! Those of you who have hearts, and therefore a wish for husbands, NEVER develop a reputation of being clever.

Train whistle.

It will put you out of the matrimonial running as though you had leprosy. If you feel a case of smart coming on, and especially if it comes with a side symptom of ugly—

DRIVER: Twenty-six miles to Gool-Gool!

SYBYLLA: **—hide your brains, cramp your minds, it is your only chance for happiness! But thankfully, I have no heart and no wish for a husband! I wish for—adventure!**

FRANK HAWDEN *appears in a buggy.*

FRANK: Miss Melvyn, I presume? I'm Frank Hawden, head jackeroo at Caddagat. Mrs Bossier sent me to fetch you from the station.

He helps SYBYLLA *onto the buggy.*

I'll try keep the horse from kicking mud on your skirts, though I daresay it won't make too much difference. So you're Mrs Bossier's granddaughter, are you?

SYBYLLA: Not remembering my own birth, I can't swear.

FRANK: Ah yes very good very good! You're not at all like your grannie. Or your aunt, Mrs Bell.

SYBYLLA: You don't think?

FRANK: They're both so good looking.

SYBYLLA: **What's this guy's deal? He's hardly an oil painting.**
Well Mr Hawden, I do value your opinion above all things.

FRANK: Ah yes you're not a bad sort, I think a fellow could have great fun with you …

SYBYLLA: **Mr Hawden was taking a year off from lording about old Britannia to man up in the colonies. He prattled on for hours—**

FRANK: And then didn't we laugh when we worked out we were cousins! Ha ha ha!

SYBYLLA: **Every few miles we passed men trudging along, going station to station looking for work, or a bite to eat.**
I wonder what disaster put those men on the road?

FRANK: Who? Oh, the tramps. Mischief of some sort. Cards, liquor. They're everywhere these days. Now, what was I saying? Oh yes— and that's why ugly girls make the best puddings, ha ha ha—

SYBYLLA: … Fascinating, Mr Hawden.

FRANK: That fence is a trifle flashy. Our neighbour, Harold Beecham, put twelve miles of it around his run, Five Bob. Do you know Harry? He's quite the swell around here—

SYBYLLA: Five Bob? That means we're almost there!

> FRANK *keeps prattling in the background as her childhood home begins to form around her.*

It had been a lifetime, but I recognised every landmark of my childhood home.

FRANK: The homestead is an hour or so from here.

SYBYLLA: **How might a great bush poet put this; shrub-lined stream among carpets of maidenhair—oooh, yes.**

FRANK: I hate this part of the journey, it's trés boring.

SYBYLLA: **The white mists crawling down the green hills, ooh words words! A-yumma yumma?**

FRANK: The trees in this country are so witchy!

SYBYLLA: **The skreel of a hundred curlews arising from the gullies!** Do you know what a curlew sounds like, Mr Hawden? A woman screaming!

> SYBYLLA *screams.* FRANK *screams. The* BALLADEERS *scream.*

FRANK: Murder birds! This country is filled with murder birds?

> *They arrive at Caddagat.*

SYBYLLA: **My grannie!**

GRANNIE: Child, you've arrived! What are these rags you're wearing— does my daughter not dress you properly?

SYBYLLA: **And my beautiful aunt, Helen! An elegant widow, like out of a novel—**

HELEN: Look how you've grown!

SYBYLLA: **My mum, but nice.**

HELEN: I'm so glad you've come. A child to warm up Caddagat again.

GRANNIE: Now, let me look at you.

SYBYLLA: Yes, Grannie.

> SYBYLLA *stands to be examined by the family, she looks about her in wonder.*

SYBYLLA: **Caddagat House was more exquisite than I remember—a roaring fire in a broad white fire place.**

GRANNIE: That mop of hair, has it ever known the companionship of a brush?

SYBYLLA: **A dining room set with gleaming silver, magazines with pictures of Paris and London strewn on the table.**

GRANNIE: Stand still, child!

SYBYLLA: Sorry, Grannie!

GRANNIE: She has excellent skin and teeth, Helen. *Something* good from her mother, I see. Nothing from her father, thank goodness.

SYBYLLA: **In the parlour, a beautiful piano, squeee! And—BOOKS! Shelves and shelves of books!**

Byron! Dickens!! Paterson! ooooh It's good to see you all again, my friends. What have I been up to? Oh, not much, just squeezing cows' teats and resenting doilies. HENRY LAWSON ERMERGHERRSH. We have not a single book in Possum Gully, Grannie! The pleasure these spines fill me with, it's so exquisite it's almost pain!

GRANNIE: Get her to bed, Helen. Her mother is right, this is going to be a big job.

> *Her mother's old bedroom.*

SYBYLLA: I get a bed all to myself. I won't miss Horace letting one rip. There's a picture of Helen at my age giving Botticelli. But I'm wrong—

HELEN: Your mum sat for that just before her wedding day.

SYBYLLA: That's Mother?

HELEN: And that one is your dad, on the same day, Prince.

> *The old nickname stops* SYBYLLA *in her tracks.*

SYBYLLA: Prince? No-one's called me that in a long time.

> SYBYLLA *starts to take deep gulps, trying to hide her face and hold back tears.*

HELEN: Poppet, why are you crying?

SYBYLLA: [*through ridic teenage tears*] **I want to tell her it's because my parents said goodbye to me like I was an unwanted guest who couldn't take the hint to leave—**

HELEN: You must be homesick.

SYBYLLA: [*through louder silly tears*] **I want to tell her it's because I'm looking at a portrait of my beautiful and hopeful Mother, before my father stole her away and failed her—**

HELEN: You must miss your dear mum terribly.

SYBYLLA: **I want to tell her it's because she's the only person who's been kind to me since I can remember, but it's none of those things—**

HELEN: Darling, tell me, what is it?

SYBYLLA: **I'M UGLY.**

HELEN: What??

SYBYLLA: **I'm ugly!**

> *She wails. Keens. Despairs. She throws herself around* HELEN'*s neck.*

Look what happened to Mother; endless work and poverty. And she was a stunner! What hope do I have?

HELEN: You're being ridiculous.

SYBYLLA: I'm ugly, and poor, and you know what's worse? I'm smart! So I have the brain to know I'm a hobgoblin. But at least I'm capable of feeling more in a day than … a ninny like pretty Gertie will feel in her entire pointless lifetime!

HELEN: Well.

SYBYLLA: See? I'm also mean.

HELEN: You don't sound very smart right now. You sound conceited.

SYBYLLA: I don't care how I sound! I take it all back, I don't care if I'm loved or not.

HELEN: Did you ever think that when you act like no-one is your equal, you might not be nice to love?

SYBYLLA: …

HELEN: Come here. Look in the mirror. What's this business? Unbrushed hair, dirty nails, ratty dress. Look how you hide yourself. You're all rah rah rah go away I don't care, but look at you—you're a scared little chicken. Don't you want to be brave and see what's underneath?

SYBYLLA: I am brave.

> Song: 'TURN AWAY FROM THE MIRROR'.

HELEN: [*singing*]

> Your reflection in the mirror is a version of you
> That reflection in the mirror is not always true
> For your eyes always look for the things that you know
> But what if those things aren't quite so?
>
> Your appearance is held hostage by what lies beneath
> Your appearance the victim, and guess who's the thief?
> You can patch up the outside but cracks lie in store
> If you don't start by fixing the floor …

Would you like my little recipe?

> Turn away from the mirror
> See yourself a little clearer
> Don't look with your eyes, surprise
> The truth you've seen is lies
> If you turn away from the mirror
> Let a truer you appear

A you that's unique, you see?
Turn away from the mirror
Let your mirror be me

Step One: No looking in the mirror for three weeks, anywhere in the house.

Step Two: brush your hair, you little troll, it looks like you've got mange.

HELEN *tickles her,* SYBYLLA *laughs.*

SYBYLLA: **A week passed, and through some kind of witchcraft, Helen began to tame my hair. How do women know how to do this secret stuff?**

HELEN *gets a basket of apples.* SYBYLLA *is writing in her journal.*

HELEN: A gift has arrived for you: fresh apples from our dear neighbour, Master Beecham of Five Bob.

SYBYLLA: Peaches last week, apples this week—Does Harold Beecham think I'm a horse?

HELEN: You are the newest filly in the shire.

SYBYLLA: With a face to match.

HELEN: God you're exhausting. Steps three through six?

SYBYLLA *is bored, goes back to writing in her journal.*

SYBYLLA: Hat in the sun, gloves in the garden—
HELEN: Head in the book—

HELEN *snatches her journal from her and reads;.*

I once put a bonnet on a stray dog and gosh we laughed. I'm expecting a similar response when Auntie finishes her ministrations.' Enough of that.
SYBYLLA: But I love writing?
HELEN: That isn't writing, it's character assassination.
[*Singing*]
You're reflected on those pages by the words that you choose
So be careful that reflection is one that won't bruise
We can work on your hair and your hands and your skin
But those words work on what lies within …

Turn away from those pages
You've been feeling low for ages

Why incite more pain? Refrain!
There's sun as well as rain
If you turn away from those pages …

I'll fight to make a girl to match the one I hope
I'll go right into battle with cream and silk and soap
But I can only win if she's fighting by my side
Not sniping from the sidelines before she's even tried
Are you with me?

SYBYLLA: **Another week passed and my hands were definitely softer. Whether it was the cold cream or just that I hadn't wrestled a pig in a while, I couldn't say.**

HELEN *presents a dress of beautiful blue fabric across her arms.*

HELEN: I've sewn you a little something, Sybby. And tonight's party for your Uncle Julius is the perfect time to show you off. Ready for the final step? Step … in.

HELEN *dresses* SYBYLLA *in a beautiful blue dress.*

[*Singing*]
It's time to look in the mirror
See yourself a little clearer
Tell me what you see—

SYBYLLA: **Evening dress is one of the most idiotic customs in existence—what could be more foolish than to endanger one's health by exposing one's chest and arms to the elements?**

She looks. She likes.

But then what could be more beautiful than a soft bosom amid a dainty nest of silk and lace …

HELEN: What do you think?

SYBYLLA: I'm hot.

HELEN: [*singing*]
What you see in the mirror
Is the girl you are to me

Ready to take the next step?

HELEN *offers her arm.*

SYBYLLA: Yes—No!—Blast it … YES.

Soiree! Whoop! The BALLADEERS *burst into Drawing Room Party Classics.* HELEN *enters, and taps a glass for formal silence.*

HELEN: Ladies and gentleman. Please may I present to you. Fresh from the wash. Ms Sybylla P Melvyn.

> SYBYLLA *enters, demurely, and curtsies low.*

GRANNIE: Lord's grace, Helen, you've performed a miracle.

> SYBYLLA *arises, sees* JAY JAY *and SCREAMS and runs at him. He grabs her and throws her over his shoulder, or into a piggy back, skirts permitting.*

JAY JAY: SYBYLLA!!

SYBYLLA: **Uncle Jay Jay, my cad of an uncle, returned from Sydney!**

JAY JAY: By George, look at you, you've turned into a wonderful-looking girl!

GRANNIE: No, Sybylla! My word! Be respectable!

JAY JAY: Look at my little prankster, Frank!

FRANK: Oh I'm looking.

JAY JAY: I could put you in my pocket!!!

SYBYLLA: **Their admiration gave me a sensation I hadn't experienced before. I didn't know whether to smile … or punch them.**

JAY JAY: Look at that, everyone, she's blushing! Lemme kiss those cheeks!

SYBYLLA: Wipe those kisses off! They're drenched with whisky and tobacco!

JAY JAY: Gammon, that's what makes 'em so nice!

HELEN: Says every heartbroken lass from here to Wagga.

JAY JAY: What can I say, I'm a generous man!

GRANNIE: Sybylla, come give Grannie a kiss.

FRANK: We doing kisses, are we?

SYBYLLA: FAMILY ONLY.

JAY JAY: I bet my boots you can't count how many boys you kissed when you were this youngster's age, Mummy. Confess, old bird!

GRANNIE: … Well when I was young…

HELEN: Oh no …

SYBYLLA: **Grannie launched into a tame anecdote that went far too long:**

GRANNIE: … and he said … 'I shall never … eat scones … AGAIN!'

She giggles and snorts.

ALL: [*forced, polite*] Ah ha. / Good one, Mum. / That was excellent.

HELEN: Where's Harry this evening?

GRANNIE: Mr Beecham shan't be joining us, he's managing the troubles on his run-up country, the drought hasn't broken there yet.

JAY JAY: You'd think the government might step up to keep the stations afloat! We made this country.

FRANK: Well, technically, we did.

Awkward moment.

But look what you've done with the place!

SYBYLLA: **We argued politics—the march towards federation!**

JAY JAY: IT WILL NEVER HAPPEN.

SYBYLLA: **Votes for women!**

FRANK: IT'S TAWDRY!

HELEN: IT'S TIME!

SYBYLLA: **I showed them my range of funny voices:**

[*Severe cockney*] Oooh oim a cockney layyydy at the marketplace!

ALL: Hahahahah!

SYBYLLA: **I was intoxicated! This was higher living!**

JAY JAY: Helen—can this striking youngster sing?

HELEN: I am yet to hear her try.

ALL: Oh yes. / Sing, Sybylla. / Give us a tight sixteen!

SYBYLLA: No! I can't, I've a horrible voice—and a cold—and influenza—and consumption—

JAY JAY: What's the point of a pretty girl if she can't entertain us! I shall start us off!

Song: 'THE CONCERT'.

[*Singing*]

There are girls who know Arabic, girls who know Greek
Girls who know poetry and when to speak
Girls who know croquet and ballet and bikes
But the best kind of girl, well, she knows what she likes …

I like a girl who knows what she likes
Who tells you without waiting what she finds so captivating
A girl who knows what she likes

Her fancies never founder when she says put fur around her
She likes a dance, especially when the music is hot
She likes a swim, especially when the water is not
I like a girl who knows what she likes
I like it when her mind's no mystery
And that girl who knows what she likes, likes me?

SYBYLLA: **Grannie did a number she warned was quite risqué!**

GRANNIE: [*singing*]
Silly Sally, careful don't slop the soup!

ALL: [*singing*]
Silly Sally, careful don't slop the soup!

SYBYLLA: **Then Frank—**

FRANK: [*singing*]
And Jesus heard the trumpets—

SYBYLLA: **Did Frank—**

FRANK: [*singing*]
The trumpets, the trumpets!
The truuuuuuuuuu—

HELEN: [*singing*]
The darkness grew and her lover was gone
In the mists of Avalon

SYBYLLA: **Helen's haunting tragedy of love and betrayal**

JAY JAY: [*steering her to stool*] Your turn, Sybylla!

SYBYLLA: No no no no no—

JAY JAY: Your turn Sybylla! Do not attempt to leave this stool until you've entertained us!

ALL: Sing sing sing sing!

FRANK: Yass Syb!

She takes a deep breath, and starts to play. It's tentative, but grows.

SYBYLLA: **This evening had been so perfect and sophisticated. I didn't want to ruin it with my loud voice and silly ideas. But I did have a little sumpthin'... that I'd been working on ...**

Song: 'IN THE WRONG KEY'.

[*Singing*]
This piano
Is tinny and out of tune

This piano
Is unpleasant to hear
This piano plays C-sharp, not C …
Like me

This piano
Is certainly out of place
This piano
Is worth less than nought
This piano
Has notes missing
Stuck pedals
Is damned hard to play
Like the girl who sits at it all day
So why do I stay?

When I write
When I play
The wrongness goes away
For a time I'm free
I'm me
And I feel
I've a voice
And a chance
And a choice
I'm the girl I'm meant to be
Not in the wrong key

If I speak of the things I hope for
The places I could go
They roll their eyes
They mock my dreams
They tell me no

If I speak of the things inside me
The girl I want to be
It's nothing they can see
So I keep it in me

But when I write
When I play
I feel that there's a way
While the song plays on
I'm gone
And the pain
In my soul
Goes away
And I'm whole
I'm the girl I'm meant to be
Not in the wrong key
And for a moment I feel I'm flying (flying, flying)
I feel my breath, I don't feel strange
And while I'm playing (I play, I play, I play!)
I'm trying … I'm trying … I'm trying to change!
To change!
Oo-oo-oh, ooh-oh!
If I find
My own voice
Take a chance
Make a choice
Play the girl I want to be
And in the right key!
The right key!

Excitement!

FRANK: God has sent us an angel!

JAY JAY: There's a fortune in that voice! Marvellous—chesty! With a little training you'd cause a sensation onstage.

FRANK: An actress?

SYBYLLA: Stop it, you're being sarcastic!

GRANNIE: Sybylla on the stage?

SYBYLLA: **Could I be an actress?**

JAY JAY: Don't you think Helen—get her up to Sydney, I could be her manager!

HELEN: Elocution and singing lessons, yes!

SYBYLLA: **I COULD be an actress!**

GRANNIE: A grand-daughter of mine! An actress—a vile, low, brazen hussy!

SYBYLLA: Granny I promise I wouldn't be a *brazen* hussy—

GRANNIE: I'd rather see her struck dead at my feet than go on the stage!

JAY JAY: Heavens, wow, that's strong.

HELEN: We could have the next Nellie Melba here, Mother!

JAY JAY: Look Mum, there's an exploded old notion about the stage being a low profession, and there are, of course, low people on the stage—

ALL: Yes, yes—that's true / I've heard some pretty bad stories … / I worked with this one actress once who—

JAY JAY: —but it would be a sin to rob Sybylla of the brilliant career she might have!

GRANNIE: Career! Career! That's all girls think of now. Gadding about, being fast, ruining themselves body and soul. Instead of being good wives and mothers as God intended!

FRANK: Hear hear.

HELEN: Mother, even good wives don't necessarily come to good.

> *Beat.*

GRANNIE: Marriage is the career we train for. No more about the den of iniquity that is the theatre.

FRANK: Hear hear.

> *Later.*

SYBYLLA: **An actress! Why didn't I think of that before? Of course I could be an actress. I mean, I've never actually seen a play but acting? It's easy, right guys?**

> BALLADEERS *look exhausted already, swigging water, eyes wide, cursing the director.*

A life on the stage—that would be a great adventure!

FRANK: I suppose you are rehearsing some more airs to show off at the next soiree.

SYBYLLA: Leave me alone, Frank!

FRANK: But then what am I to do with it?

SYBYLLA: Do with what?

FRANK: My love!

SYBYLLA: Whaaaaaaaa?

FRANK: Prepare yourself. When I'm twenty-four I'll come into my property in England and I want to take you back there with me. I simply can't wait to present you to daddy … he'll be FURIOUS. What are you laughing at?

SYBYLLA: You want me to marry you??!! Frank, you are something!

FRANK: Ah, that's what it is. You don't think you're good enough.

Song: 'BRICK'.

Sybylla, let me be frank. Frank? Get it?

FRANK *grabs the mic.*

SYBYLLA: **Sorry, what? He's getting a song?**

FRANK: [*singing*]

> I was a fool when I saw your face
> I put pretty way too high and to my damned disgrace
> I've gone and made you doubt that we can ever work it out
> It's a pity cos you're pretty fine I got no doubt, that
> You're better than a beauty
> Beauty doesn't stick
> You're cooler than a cutie
> You cut and gut me quick
> Syb, you're a squib
> And you make my stomach sick
> You're better than a beauty baby
> You're a brick

SYBYLLA: I'm a brick?

FRANK: Hear me out!

[*Singing*]

> You're solid and reliable
> You hold your ground
> And not even a bushfire
> Could burn you down
> And though you're kinda tiny
> I'd never let you fall
> Cos baby don't you realise
> Two bricks make a wall
> Let's make a wall!

Cos you're better than a beauty
Beauty doesn't stick
And you're cooler than a cutie
You cut and gut me quick
Hon, you're so fun
That I laugh until I'm sick
You're better than a beauty, baby
Better than a beauty, baby …

You're better than a beauty
Beauty doesn't stick
And you're cooler than a cutie
You cut and gut me quick
So, don't say no
Or I'll seriously be sick
You're better than a beauty
Baby, you're a brick

He kneels and takes her hand. SYBYLLA *grabs the mic back off him.*

SYBYLLA: **Alright, they're MY band.**

Song: 'GOOD ENOUGH'.

[*Singing*]

You're looking at me
But you're not looking at me
You're saying words about another girl
Maybe a girl I'd like to be
Maybe a girl I'd just like
But not the girl you see
So I strike

She clocks him one, or trips him over to the ground.

Don't look at me that way
You think I like that stuff?
With every word you say
You're not good enough
Not good enough

FRANK: Spicy!

SYBYLLA: [*singing*]
> I'm here for me okay?
> If you don't like that, tough
> Now get the hell away
> You're not good enough
> Nowhere near good enough

FRANK: Be sensible! I know who you are and I don't mind one bit.

SYBYLLA: [*singing*]
> You're talking at me
> But you're not talking to me
> Am I a space you think you have to fill?
> A space to see yourself appear?
> A space to show you 'you'?
> Well there's no space in here
> Not for two
>
> Don't talk to me that way
> As if it's harmless fluff
> The words you choose to say
> Are not good enough
> Not good enough

SYBYLLA *threatens him again.*

> Why do you stand and stay?
> You want to call my bluff?
> Talk till your hair is grey
> You're not good enough
> Nowhere near good enough

FRANK *flees.* GRANNIE *arrives.*

GRANNIE: Sybylla! Mr Hawden has complained of your conduct. He says you have been flirting with him?

SYBYLLA: That little rat-faced man.

GRANNIE: A woman must never flirt. And he wants to marry you, what say you?

SYBYLLA: I don't love him, Grannie!

GRANNIE: That's hardly the point.

SYBYLLA: I wouldn't even lower myself to marry the King of England!

GRANNIE: Well the King hasn't enquired. But Mr Hawden has. He comes from a very distinguished family. It would be a secure life every girl would be grateful for.

SYBYLLA: Marriage is not fair to women, Grannie, come on—it sucks!

GRANNIE: Marriage gives us respectability.

SYBYLLA: That's just what men want us to think!

GRANNIE: [*exiting*] There is no other respectable way.

SYBYLLA: Grannie, I will make a way!

[*Singing*]

> He wants to pick me off the shelf
> He doesn't even see my self
> A self I've barely seen
> He's in the market, I'm the mare
> He'll ride me off to who-knows-where
> Maybe it's mean
> But his manner and his motives make me scream …
> They're obscene!

> Don't make me be that way
> Don't want to be so tough
> If I believed I'd pray
> It'd be good enough
> Just good enough

> But I'll never be that way
> I know it's weird and rough
> It's not a part that I can ever play
> It's so not good enough
> It will never be good enough
> Nowhere near good enough!

Caddagat Orchard. SYBYLLA *in her old Possum Gully mop clothes under a tree.*

SYBYLLA: **Girls! Those of you who wish for happiness, and therefore husbands—WHY! Marriage is the most horribly tied-down unfair-to-women existence going!**

Now I could get back to the real business of living—ordering uncle to bring the latest books back from Sydney, then sprawling

**under a tree in the orchard to devour both them and ripe apple.
I know this kind of thing got Eve in trouble, but a little bit of
knowledge never did me any harm. But first: My Gertie.**

'My dearest Gertie. I have started to write no less than seven
letters to send you, but something always interrupts me—'

HELEN: Sybbbby! Get some apples for the kitchen please!

SYBYLLA *climbs an apple tree.*

SYBYLLA: 'Living at Caddagat is lovely! Uncle Jay thinks he runs the
place, but Grannie is the actual boss. One of my duties is to assist
her with the accounts, and write her business letters.'

JAY JAY: Has anyone seen my hat?

SYBYLLA: 'Another duty is to find Uncle Jay Jay's hat when he mislays
it. Which is about ten times a day.'
It's on your head!

JAY JAY: So it is.

She takes the hat and puts it upon her own head.

SYBYLLA: 'My main duty is to attend the tramps. No man is a refused a
bite to eat at Caddagat. Poor souls, with their futile quest for work.'
Uncle, couldn't we find work for the tramps here?

JAY JAY: Work?! That's the very thing those bums are terrified they
might get.

SYBYLLA: Couldn't we make a new law to help them?

JAY JAY: Put on one of your funny voices.

SYBYLLA: [*Irish*] 'Tis an unfair plight that some have nought while
others live the life of Riley.

JAY JAY: Wonderful, yes!

SYBYLLA: If us squatters hadn't taken so much land to begin with,
there'd be plenty—

JAY JAY: So I'm supposed to share Caddagat with those lazy devils and
have a only piece for myself? We've got a socialist in our midst!
With the flies, and the tramps, and a pesky thing called Sybylla
asking questions, a man's life's not worth living.

SYBYLLA *starts to climb the ladder to pick the apples up the tree.*

SYBYLLA: 'If men insist on running everything, they should do
something better with it, Gertie. But women are too tied up being
milk machines to get in there and fix it … Everything's so unfair

I don't even know who to yell at—the iron hand of inequality has settled down upon us. Hmmmm I sound clever … '

Jay Jay?

HARRY *enters.*

Do you tink I could be a politician??

HARRY: I'd vote for you.

> SYBYLLA *gets a fright, squeals and slips.* HARRY *catches her. The apples spill everywhere.*

I just saved your life.

> SYBYLLA *is shocked into silence to be so manhandled by a stranger.*

I haven't seen you before. Do you work in the kitchen? You've probably heard of me … I'm a pretty big deal round here. Own some land and stuff.

SYBYLLA: **Harold. Beecham.**

> *Sybby stays in character.*

Let me go this instant, sir. It's lucky women don't have the right to vote, cos I wouldn't vote for you! Staring up women's skirts.

> *He puts her down.*

HARRY: Don't I get a kiss?

SYBYLLA: What for?

HARRY: I'm a hero, you could have died.

SYBYLLA: If the missus catches me, you'll get me fired.

HARRY: Then we could run away together.

> *He comes close to her.* SYBYLLA *gets a lil hot 'n' confused 'n' bewildered.*

SYBYLLA: … h … ts … gehh … mmm …

HARRY: [*laughing*] Don't worry, I never kiss girls … well, not against their will.

SYBYLLA: You better pick up these apples, or I'll tell the missus I've been harassed by some weirdo in the orchard.

HARRY: You're very brave, aren't you.

SYBYLLA: … h … ts … Yes.

HARRY: Stand still, let's see what you've got.

He gets out his horse whip, moves back a distance, and cracks it near SYBYLLA. *She doesn't flinch.*

Farrrrr out! Not so much as blinked an eyelash! Thoroughbred.

SYBYLLA: Pick 'em up.

HARRY *hesitates.*

HARRY: Yes ma'am. What's your name then?

He starts collecting the fruit. HELEN, JAY JAY *and* GRANNIE *bustle in.*

HELEN: Sybylla, where are those apples?—Harold? Harold's arrived!

JAY JAY: What are you doing down there, old cock?

GRANNIE: Harold! What's news from upcountry?

HELEN: I see you've finally met our Sybylla!

HARRY *is frozen in horror.*

SYBYLLA: Mr Beecham? Heavens, I had no idea! Aunt Helen, this kind gentleman was just helping me pick up these apples I so clumsily dropped.

HARRY: Um yeah, I was just … helping.

GRANNIE: Harry you look flushed, are you feeling unwell?

HARRY: … h … ts … gehh … mmm …

HELEN: Gracious, Mother, you're right.

She places her palm on his forehead.

Harold, you've gone bright red.

HARRY: … h … ts … Yes.

HARRY *stares at* SYBYLLA, *speechless.*

HELEN: Oh, my … I think I can smell something burning. In the kitchen.

GRANNIE: What!? Oh! Yes, fire, I can smell fire, let us investigate.

JAY JAY: Fire, what?

HELEN: Come, Jay Jay, let's see what that burning smell is.

JAY JAY: I can't smell a goddamn thing, what are you women on about?

HELEN *and* GRAN: Shutup.

HELEN *bundles them quickly off.*

SYBYLLA: Do shake hands. I always shake hands with anyone I think
   I'll like.
HARRY: Pon my honour, Miss Melvyn, I had no idea it was you—
SYBYLLA: Whereas if I were a kitchen maid … ?
HARRY: I've never done that before, I … I feel this game isn't very fair.
SYBYLLA: Life is never fair for the *fairer* sex, now you know what it
   feels like.
HARRY: Hmmm, a very interesting subject to learn more about. Hey,
   why don't you come by Five Bob for a bit? Stay with me and the
   Aunties. You could teach me more.
SYBYLLA: And what'll I learn?
HARRY: How to crack a whip.

   He does so again, then doffs his hat.

Ms Melvyn.

   Exits. Hot. Bam.

Five Bob. SYBYLLA *and* HARRY *float in on an adorb boat down the
river.* HARRY *strums the guitar.*

Song: 'WAIT WITH YOU'.

SYBYLLA: **Harold Beecham. Giver of apples. Taker of whatever he
   wants. He has an air of If-people-fail-they-must-have-brought-
   it-on-themselves about him. I had finally found a career worthy
   of my talents—bringing this conceited stallion dooooowwwn.**
HARRY: [*singing*]
          Is it too late?
          It feels so early
          Time seems to wait
          While I wait with you
          Is it my fate
          To be caught by your words?
          So I'll wait, I'll wait with you
SYBYLLA: Awfully kind of you to have hosted me for the month, Mr
   Beecham. Pray tell, how many girls have you trapped with this boat
   and song bit?
HARRY: Dozens upon dozens. But you're not like the other girls.
SYBYLLA: Oh?

HARRY: You're not a girl, you're a nightmare.

>SYBYLLA *gasps.*

SYBYLLA: Oh! You say all the right things.
HARRY: [*singing*]
>>Will you come home?
>>Or have you already?
>>Home seems at hand
>>While I wait with you

SYBYLLA: Can you at least sing in tune, Harry?
HARRY: [*singing*]
>>It seems my fate

SYBYLLA: The frogs think it's a mating call.
HARRY: [*singing*]
>>To be home in your heart
>>So I'll wait, I'll wait with you

SYBYLLA: Do you know anything less sentimental?
HARRY: What's the matter, you having feelings?
SYBYLLA: Yes. I'm feeling bored.
HARRY: Do you ever not say what you think?
SYBYLLA: Do you ever think?
HARRY: Clearly not, I'm trapped up creek with a madwoman.

>SYBYLLA *laughs. She leans over the edge of the boat,* HARRY *responds, unflapped.*

HARRY: Don't lean over the edge—
SYBYLLA: *Pourquoi*?
HARRY: If you fall in the river, I'll be forced to save you again.
SYBYLLA: I'd rather die than give you that satisfaction.
HARRY: [*singing*]
>>Where will you go?

SYBYLLA: [*leaning*] Harry …
HARRY: [*singing*]
>>I feel you departing
>>Though you're just there
>>While I wait with you
>>Was it my fate

SYBYLLA: I'm *leeaanning* …

HARRY: [*singing*]
> To be lost and found … ?
> To be found then lost?
> Still I wait, I wait with you
> And I'll wait, I'll wait with you

Sybylla, I'm going to Melbourne for a few weeks. When I return, may I visit you?

> *She clocks his question. It's too real. She stands up in the boat, and goes to jump.*

Sybylla, please, don't!

> *She stops. Someone cared enough to try stop her. He gets up to steady her. They rock for a moment, then together—*

BOTH: [*singing*]
> I'll wait with you …

> *He leans in for … a kiss?—but instead she drags him over the edge.* BALLADEERS *make sound of water splashing as the kookaburras peal in laughter.*

Days later at Caddagat. SYBYLLA *fizzes around her room, nattering at* HELEN.

SYBYLLA: Harry dragged me up onto the riverbank and kept saying 'You could have died, you could have died!' Hahahaha!

HELEN: Yes, you've told me this one before.

SYBYLLA: I got him, Helen! I got him gooood! He was way less conceited soaking wet and covered in mud! His clothes were all … stuck to his skin, he looked … soo so stupid! His shirt went all see-through?

HELEN: Did it.

SYBYLLA: Yep.

> He's bigger than you think.

HELEN: Is he.

SYBYLLA: Yep. His arms are like, whoa. You wouldn't think it in those suits. He's so … sturdy. [*Gesturing with her hands*] Thick.

HELEN: Right. And your clothes? Were you proper?

SYBYLLA: [*laughing*] … I looked down and they were all clinging to me. And Harry turned around. So I turned around.

And I said 'got yoooou'. And ran.

HELEN: …

Sybylla, do you know what you're doing?

SYBYLLA: What do you mean?

HELEN: When Harry proposes. Will you say yes?

SYBYLLA: Harry's not going to propose to someone like me! We're just great friends?

HELEN: Who you choose to marry is the most important decision of your life—

SYBYLLA: Well I wouldn't choose Harry. He's so … [*Gesturing the thick gesture again*] … arrogant! He thinks he could have any woman for the asking.

HELEN: The family will think it a good match.

SYBYLLA: Why does it always come back to marriage! You haven't married again, and now you live however you like. That's what I choose, too.

HELEN: Sybylla, I'm not a widow.

SYBYLLA: What?

HELEN: My husband is alive and living with another woman. He married me and swept me away, but after a year, he 'tired' of me, and abandoned me for his mistress. And here I am, an embarrassment to the family.

SYBYLLA: An embarrassment?

I wanted to scream at her—why is it the religion of the world to blame the woman! He's the embarrassment! But I could see Helen wore this wound like it was all that was left of her.

But now … you're free! You're free, Helen!

HELEN: No. I'm not a wife. I'm not a widow. I'm nothing. There's no place for a woman who's been cast aside. Your mother and I were rebellious, just like you—we thought we were audacious marrying for love rather than practicality. But we chose poorly.

Harry is kind and gentle. You won't find a man more true to secure you.

GRANNIE *calls from off and comes in.*

GRANNIE: Ladies! The Beechams are a holding a ball Satd'y week!

HELEN *starts to dress* SYBYLLA *in evening gown.*

SYBYLLA: Harry has returned from Melbourne?

GRANNIE: Harry has been back for weeks, child.

SYBYLLA: **Weeks?**

GRANNIE: Prepare the warpaint and armour ladies!

SYBYLLA: **Harry has been back for weeks?**

HELEN: I've made you a lovely dress for Beecham Ball, Sybylla.

SYBYLLA: **And he hasn't come and seen me?**

HELEN: White lace and ribbon.

SYBYLLA: **What could be occupying his time?**

BLANCHE DERRICK *sweeps into the Beecham Ball in a stunning dress of feathers.* HARRY *and she promenade around the dance floor, total A-listers.* SYBYLLA *enters in a simple white dress.*

HARRY: Ladies and gentleman, what an honour to host the best of the district at our annual Beecham Ball! Now may I—

Someone whispers to HARRY*, and hands him a note to read.*

Whoever owns the red carriage with the two clydesdales and the gold trimmings, your carriage is blocking the driveway, thank you.

Now, may I present our special guest, the belle of the ball, all the way from Melbourne: Ms Blanche Derrick!

Everyone applauds.

JAY JAY: How do you do, Ms Derrick.

BLANCHE: How do you doooo.

FRANK: What part of Melbourne do you hail from, Ms Derrick?

BLANCHE: Tooooorak.

HARRY: Yes, she's from the good part.

ALL: Oh thank goodness. / Phew. / Yes Southside is better.

SYBYLLA *enters in a white lace dress.*

SYBYLLA: **Beecham Ball …**

She clocks the men all around BLANCHE.

… where every farmer wants a wife.

HARRY: Sybby! Ms Derrick, this is Ms Melvyn.

BLANCHE: Hhhhhhhoow do you doooo.

SYBYLLA: I'm gooooooooooo. Are you staying with Mr Beecham at Five Bob?

BLANCHE: Yisssssss. I am! He's kindly invited me to tour his estates. Today he took me on the loveliest boat ride.

SYBYLLA: He took you on the boat? You poor thing.

BLANCHE: I love your dress. Were those doilies?

SYBYLLA: I love your dress. Was that a whole chicken?

BLANCHE: Hhhhahhhahhow funnay. Harry, I love country people! I could totally live like this. Come, let's dance!

> He takes BLANCHE *back to the dance floor. The guests surround* BLANCHE, *who has taken the centre of the ballroom floor.*
>
> Song: 'MAKE A SUCCESS'.

ALL: [*singing*]
> B-b-b-blanche
> B-b-b-blanche

BLANCHE: [*singing*]
> Keep yourself nice, my nan used to say
> But nice gets you nothing and nowhere today
> Nice is alright for a hat or a dress
> But I'd rather make a mess
> Don't be too loud, is the constant refrain
> And keep your future free of a single stain
> Stains are for someone else to get clean
> And I'd rather be a queen
> I make my way around in the latest dress
> I make them give me more, I won't settle for less
> I make them all oblige my inherent noblesse
> I make it clear I'm here to make—

ALL: [*singing*]
> To make? To make?

BLANCHE: [*singing*]
> To make a success!
> I'm here to make a suc—, make-make a success!

ALL: [*singing*]
> She's/I'm here to make a suc—, make-make a success!

> FRANK *saunters up to* SYBYLLA.

FRANK: I've heard it said she's one of the greatest beauties of Melbourne.

SYBYLLA: I've heard it said Melbourne's a hole of a town.

FRANK: Splendid creature …

SYBYLLA: Oh yes. Splendid. I bet she never bothers anyone with silly ideas and never acts with impropriety. I bet she lives in a sea of unruffled self-confidence and would never let her emotions run away with her, BECAUSE SHE HAS NO EMOTIONS.

FRANK: Sybylla?

SYBYLLA: SHUT UP FRANK.

> *The dance continues.*

BLANCHE: [*singing*]
>> Suffer and smile, go on, just force it
>> The only suffering worth it are these heels and this corset
>> Some old guy said that pain's a woman's lot
>> But I'd really rather not
>> I make it kind of tough for men I must confess
>> I make it known how much it takes to get me to yes
>> I make the most of every single gift I possess
>> I hope it's clear I'm here to make—

ALL: [*singing*]
>> To make? To make?

BLANCHE: [*singing*]
>> To make a success!

ALL: [*singing*]
>> That's how you make a suc— make-make a success!
>> That's how you make a suc— make-make a success!

> BLANCHE *beelines for* SYBYLLA.

BLANCHE: Gosh it's fun, isn't it?

SYBYLLA: Making a success? I wouldn't know.

BLANCHE: Shopping for husbands. I've been auditioning the whole Eastern seaboard. Look at them—sweaty little boys, panting for attention.

> *She looks back at the sweaty chorus of men, sweating, breathing heavily from the dance, doing small step-togethers while holding their instruments, awaiting her return.*

Back in a minute, gents!

MEN: [*panting*] Okay, Blanche!

BLANCHE: Who's on your to-do list? [*Looking at* FRANK] That little skinny one isn't awful—

SYBYLLA: Oh no. He's awful. But me? No list. No to-do-ing.

BLANCHE: Don't deny yourself the fun of the chase, darling! You should come to Melbourne, we'll run amok— [*Intimately*] Are you a terror? I bet you're a terror.

SYBYLLA: [*entranced*] I don't know what I am.

BLANCHE: We must find out before you get hitched!

SYBYLLA: Will it be fun … when you do get hitched?

BLANCHE: It's all good game, Sybylla. Tell a boy yes then work out the details later. A gal's got to eat—does it matter how she gets a seat at the table?

> HARRY *returns, sees them laughing together.*

HARRY: Ripper, you're getting on! I told Blanche you were the best gal around. Come on Syb, let's dance.

> SYBYLLA *tentatively takes* HARRY*'s hand.* BLANCHE *moves on.*

BLANCHE: [*singing*]
> I make the magazines with every evening dress
> I make a conquest with a tiny caress
> I make it my mission, but nevertheless
> I'm out when there's no way to make

ALL: [*singing*]
> To make? To make?

BLANCHE: [*singing*]
> To make a success!

ALL: [*singing*]
> That's how you make a suc— make-make a success!
> That's how you make a suc— make-make a success!

> *The party fades as* SYBYLLA *and* HARRY *walk into the orchard garden on the hot summer night.*

HARRY: Blanche is …

SYBYLLA: … incandescent. Like a firework made human.

HARRY: You're a pair of sparklers.

Awkward moment. HARRY *clears his throat, removes his hat and riding crop, wipes his sweaty palms on his trousers and prepares himself.*

Well. Ahem. It's no use making a long yarn about nothing. I'm sure you know what I want to say better than I do myself. Tell me, will it be yes or no?

SYBYLLA: What … is the question?

He laughs, a bit loud.

HARRY: You know what I've been going to ask since I first clapped eyes on you. I don't want to hurry you, only I want you to be engaged to me for safety.

SYBYLLA: Engaged?

HARRY: I didn't think it wise to dawdle.

SYBYLLA: Oh.

uMm …

Yes.

HARRY: Yes?

SYBYLLA: I'll ah … be engaged … to you?

HARRY: Oh! Good!

He laughs joyously.

Ha! I didn't think you'd say yes so easy, like any other girl. Thought you'd pick a fight first!

That's that then—

HARRY *takes her face to kiss it.* SYBYLLA *snatches his riding crop and brings it with all her strength across his face. He grabs her wrist fiercely.*

A less stinging rebuke would have done the job.

SYBYLLA: I … Harry …

He lets her wrist go. She holds her bruising flesh.

HARRY: I'm sorry. That was my fault. I thought I could steal a kiss from my future wife. You okay?

He looks at her wrist, she nods. He tries to get a smile from her. She can't form words.

I've never seen you speechless. It's quite peaceful. How about that dance, Ms Melvyn?

She wordlessly obliges, they hold each other cautiously, formally, and dance in place to sound of the BALLADEERS.

SYBYLLA: **I hit him. What an unwomanly thing to do. I never know what women are supposed to do. I can feel his heart beating in his chest. That … was my proposal? My brilliant proposal. Delivered like an invitation to a picnic. Not at all like I'd read about in books.**

She buries her face into his chest in embarrassment. HARRY *takes it as affection, grows confident in their dance, and lets it grow.* SYBYLLA *follows along, helplessly.*

'Like any other girl!' How dare he?! … so … why does he like me? I'm erratic. I'm a pest. I have none of the virtues which men want in a wife. He must be dim.

Great hair though.

HARRY: Oh I nearly forgot.

He pulls away from the dance, takes a ring box from his pocket.

SYBYLLA: **Wait wait wait wait wait this is not a romance!**

On bended knee. He opens the box, presents a sparkling diamond ring.

THIS IS NOT A ROMANCE!

HARRY: Let's see if it fits.

SYBYLLA: Don't put it on! That would make it … real.

HARRY: This isn't real?

SYBYLLA: Give me three months! Three months probation.

HARRY: I knew you'd be unorthodox!

He stays on bended knee staring at her expectantly. For too long. He doesn't know what to do.

Soooooooooo. What do we do in the meantime?

SYBYLLA: Just be—Harry! I'll be Sybylla, just as before. Normal. Get up, I can't bear it.

HARRY: But take the ring and wear it, won't you?

She eyes it aghast.

SYBYLLA: Damn. It's very beautiful isn't it.

She yells to the BALLADEERS*:*

IT'S A GREAT RING GUYS.

No Harry, this is a beautiful ring for a beautiful woman, you're making a mistake.

HARRY: Shut up, you goose. Put it on.

> HARRY *slips the ring onto her finger. He twirls her back into dancing, this time they start to get real good together, Fred and Shabby Chic Ginger.* SYBYLLA *looks to the heavens—an intense sunrise begins to take over the horizon, the strains of the Balladeeers' music swells with tortured romantic beauty.*

Look—the sun's rising.

SYBYLLA: **Oh NO, are you joking. LOOK—My dear fellow Australians! A trash sunrise!**

> *She points at the band—*

You guys aren't helping!

> *They shrug and keep summoning the sun's rays. She concedes.*

HOW ROMANTIC.

> HARRY *take her face again, searching for whether he'll get another slap.* SYBYLLA *stays still. He kisses her. Her first kiss. She is breathless and stunned and embarrassed and entranced. He turns to watch the sunrise. She looks down at her ring, then looks back to us, opens her mouth to say something—but she's speechless.*

> *Blackout.*

END OF ACT ONE

ACT TWO

The BALLADEERS *pound out folk romps as the sun blazes down.*
SYBYLLA *wears a razzed-up birthday frock, an opulent hat that doesn't
sit right, looking ever closer to the Lady of Five Bob, and not quite
herself. She's uncomfortable and bloody hot. She's pounding the keys,
looking the life of the party.*

SYBYLLA: **My dear fellow Australians.**
   Hi.
   How's this band?
   How are you going?
   Great!
   How am I going?

   Points at her ring.

Got a ring on it.
   Pretty weird.

   She stares at the ring, twisting it round and round. HARRY
   appears in a buggy, and whispers:

HARRY: Hurry Mrs Harold Beecham, you'll be late for your birthday
   picnic.
SYBYLLA: Don't call me that, people will hear you!
HARRY: Sorry, Mrs Harold Beecham. It's a good name for you. Suits
   you.
SYBYLLA: Let me drive—
HARRY: Just sit back, Sybby.

   She sits back, perturbed.

SYBYLLA: **I loved riding horses. By the age ten, Father had taught
   me to ride everything. Side-saddle, man-saddle, no-saddle,
   astride! 'She's a tomboy!' Mother would cry. 'Let her alone!'
   Father would say.**

   You're going too slow, Harry!

HARRY: Let me drive.

SYBYLLA: **Little boys dream of becoming bushrangers, train drivers—nothing so garishly simple for me. I dreamed that when I grew up, I would ride my horse around the world and find and save all the sick and starving babies. Carry old useless people into shelters. Make sure all animals were fat and happy. I even thought I could stop people plucking flowers against their wishes.**

Gah-gah gah-gah gah- gah gah- gah gah-gah gah- gah gah-GAH! Here comes Sybylla to save the babies and the flowers!

HARRY: Sybby, sit down, what are you doing?

SYBYLLA: **Once upon a time when the days were long and hot; I, Sybylla Melvyn, was in a buggy being driven to my seventeenth birthday party.**

I was all grown up, and I did not ride my horse around the world. I sat. Still. Next to a man and enjoyed the view …

A man with ambitions to change the world is a curse to himself, but a woman? She's not just a creature out of place. She has no place. A girl with dreams is a lonely thing.

HARRY: Here we are!

SYBYLLA: **I guess it was a little less lonely …**

The family picnic begins to arrive.

HELEN: Here's the lovely pair!

SYBYLLA: **This story is not going quite how I planned.**

JAY JAY: Happy birthday, young lady!

SYBYLLA: **I'm not really engaged. It's probation.**

HARRY: Allow me, my lady.

He helps her out of the buggy, and stands her by his side.

SYBYLLA: **I'm just trying out what it is to have a place by someone's side.**

FRANK: Happy birthday, Sybby!

HARRY: Hip hip—

ALL: Hooray!

Her Caddagat family, HARRY *and* FRANK *desert the* BALLADEERS *and surround her, yelling Happy Birthday!* HELEN *lays out a picnic rug around a startled* SYBYLLA. JAY JAY *carries a birthday present.* FRANK *skips, holding champagne bottles.*

FRANK: Birthday bumps! Everyone on a corner!

FRANK *helps* HELEN *spread out the rug.*

Seventeen bumps in the air plus one for luck!

SYBYLLA *climbs onto the rug in delight, They start to toss her high in the air, she squeals with delight.*

ALL: One! Two! Three—

GRANNIE *enters with the birthday cake.*

GRANNIE: Sybylla Penelope Melvyn, you shameful hussy!

They all put her down and look abashed and cheeky with shame.

JAY JAY: Shoosh you old duck, it's tradition!

GRANNIE: She's seventeen, she's a woman now, she cannot climb about like a boy.

HELEN: Mother, you're being boring.

JAY JAY *and* FRANK: [*chanting*] BOOOOOORING! BOOOOORING!

GRANNIE: There are things she simply cannot do anymore.

HARRY: [*mimicking* GRANNIE] She simply cannot have fun anymore!

FRANK: I want a turn!

FRANK *gets scared.*

No no, stop, I'm scared, I've lost confidence.

All are disappointed.

JAY JAY: Open your present, Syb!

SYBYLLA *pulls out a doll from the gift box.*

SYBYLLA: A gift! Uncle Jay Jay, thank you! … A doll?

JAY JAY: You can play with the dolly rather than worry your nog with tramps and politics and [*funny voice*] economic prosperity for all.

SYBYLLA: Am I a well-behaved woman, or a little girl playing dolly today? Can someone tell me the rules? Here Frank, dolly make you feel better.

FRANK: Thank you, she's stunning. Sweet Seventeen, never been kissed?

SYBYLLA: Um … No!

SYBYLLA *blushes crimson and stares stupidly at* HARRY.

FRANK: Is she ticklish?

SYBYLLA: No!

HELEN: Yes she is. Very.

SYBYLLA: NO!

> *He tickles* SYBYLLA *with the doll's hands, she squeals, very VERY ticklish.*

FRANK: Oh yes! The birthday girl is ticklish!

SYBYLLA: No stop! I HATE IT I HATE IT I HATE IT.

FRANK: No-one can save you from the dolly!

> *They roll around on the picnic rug,* FRANK *pinning her with the doll and tickling her, childish pealing laughter.* HARRY *grabs at* FRANK *roughly and pulls him off her.*

HARRY: Get off her!

> *Tense pause,* HARRY, *embarrassed, stalks off.* SYBYLLA *follows after a beat.*

SYBYLLA: Harry?

FRANK: [*in sing song, using the doll as puppet*] Uh oh, he's been stu-hunng! But by whhhhat!

> *He starts to tickle* JAY JAY.

A-tickle tickle tickle tickle—

JAY JAY: Fuck off Frank.

> SYBYLLA *follows after a stormy* HARRY. *She's exhilarated.*

HARRY: Explain yourself to me!

SYBYLLA: Excuse me?

HARRY: Explain your conduct with other men to my satisfaction.

SYBYLLA: You explain your conduct to me! I can behave as I please without your permission!

HARRY: I could have any woman wear that ring, a woman who doesn't go out of her way to embarrass me like you do.

> *She drags off the ring.*

SYBYLLA: Here you go then, sir! I will wear your ring, NO MORE! I never had the slightest intention of marrying you!

HARRY: What?

SYBYLLA: I said yes to teach you a lesson, Harold Beecham! That everyone wants you for your money, not your conceited mug and the weak things inside it! WEAK WEAK WEAK.

HARRY: …

Are you in earnest?

SYBYLLA: Go get yourself a beautiful *useful* woman, Harry. One that knows how to cook pies and stuff. Don't bother with me, I'm too silly.

HARRY: I thought you were different. I thought you were a woman a man could stake his life on.

SYBYLLA: And I thought you were a man who wouldn't try to own me. I am not your property.

HARRY: …

I would never try to—

But you're my—

You should behave as you like. Goodbye, Ms Melvyn.

He turns to leave.

SYBYLLA: Harry—please, wait. I'm sorry. I said crappy things.

HARRY: Did you mean them?

SYBYLLA: Of course I didn't. Did you mean what you said?

HARRY: No—

SYBYLLA: Did you mean the name Mrs Harold Beecham suited me?

HARRY: … What?

SYBYLLA: Let me drive the horses?

HARRY: … this is about horses??

SYBYLLA: Let's go back to before. When we were mates. And I made you laugh, and you liked me tormenting you.

HARRY: Mates?

SYBYLLA: Yes.

HARRY: God, Syb, you … (drive me insane).

Song: 'A LITTLE BIT MORE'.

[*Singing*]

You get me feeling stuck-stuck-stuck in a tree

And you scramble down-down so you can laugh at me

You get me-get me in a state

You reckon-reckon-reckon that makes you a mate?
You're a mosquito buzz-buzz-buzzin' round my head
But I can't slap-slap-slap-slap you dead
Cos your bite-bite-bite feels so great
I reckon-reckon-reckon that don't make you a mate

But still I stay out in the sun, un
Till we burn, and call it fun, and
See what sort of trouble waits in
Store—for mates
Mates and a little bit more

SYBYLLA: More? You've never even mentioned love.

HARRY: I'm scared—

SYBYLLA: Spare me, a man scared to show feelings!

HARRY: I'm *scared* you'll hit me.

> *She goes to hit him, he catches her arm and spins her round.*

Will you wear my ring again?

SYBYLLA: [*singing*]

Would you try to make a foal run before it could walk?
Would you debate the vote before a baby could talk?
Would you force a seedling out from under the ground?
You could try but you'll be disappointed I've found
Would you wait a while, combine romance and reason?
Would a farmer fertilise if it wasn't the season?
If you pluck the grapes too early from the vine
You'll get vinegar instead of wine

And will you stay out in the sun
Until we burn, and call it fun?
And see what sort of trouble waits in store
—For mates

HARRY: [*singing*]

Mates and a little bit more

SYBYLLA: [*singing*]

A little bit more?

HARRY: [*singing*]

A little bit more

SYBYLLA: [*singing*]
> A little bit more …

HARRY: [*singing*]
> A little bit—

SYBYLLA: [*singing*]
> Mates?

HARRY: [*singing*]
> Mates?

SYBYLLA: [*singing*]
> Mates

BOTH: [*singing*]
> Mates

HARRY: [*singing*]
> And a little bit more—

SYBYLLA: [*singing*]
> A little bit more?

HARRY: [*singing*]
> A little bit more

SYBYLLA: [*singing*]
> A little bit more …

HARRY: [*singing*]
> A little bit—

SYBYLLA: [*singing*]
> Mates?

HARRY: [*singing*]
> Mates?

SYBYLLA: [*singing*]
> Mates

BOTH: [*singing*]
> Mates …

SYBYLLA: [*singing*]
> And a little bit more

HARRY: I have thought of nothing but you day and night since I clapped eyes on you up that tree. I love you, Sybylla. Do you love me?

SYBYLLA: …

HARRY: You hesitated! Far out, you hesitated!

SYBYLLA: Harry I … ! I very nearly love you—

HARRY: That doesn't sound great.

SYBYLLA: Don't hurry me! I feel like I know nothing about anything but everyone wants me to know *something* and all I know is I want everything and I can't work out what that is!

HARRY: What does that mean?

> *She hits him but he catches her hand and holds it to his heart.*

[*Singing*]

> So I end up feeling stuck-stuck-stuck in that tree
> While you're skit-skit-skitting round making fun of me
> I guess this, guess this, is our natural state?

SYBYLLA: [*singing*]

> You reckon-reckon-reckon you can handle that, mate?

HARRY: I do.

[*Singing*]

> And so I'll stay out in the sun, un
> Till we burn, and call it fun, and
> See what sort of trouble waits in store—for mates
> Mates and a little bit more
> I'll stay out in the sun … [*etc.*]

> HARRY *repeats as* SYBYLLA *sings over the top—*

SYBYLLA: [*singing*]

> Wait a while, combine romance and reason
> Fertilise, when it's the season
> Pluck the grapes, when they're ready
> Walk with me, nice and slow and steady

> *They both 'doo-doo' their counter melodies, slowly working towards unison and then … a kiss?*

SYBYLLA: **Harry and I went back on probation. But as the three month deadline drew close, and the apple trees began to shed their leaves, I was no closer to committing to a choice. But then, of course, a fateful letter changed my fate again … which is why they're called fateful.**

GRANNIE: Sybylla!

> GRANNIE *arrives with a letter.* SYBYLLA *begins to read.*

SYBYLLA: **A letter from my mother, written in a steel that cut into my soul:**

I won't go! I can't! I won't!

GRANNIE: Your mother has given her word.

SYBYLLA: She's done it deliberately, Grannie! She knows I would rather die than be a governess! Helen!!

HELEN *enters.*

GRANNIE: Lucy has written. Her husband has taken a loan from a neighbour and cannot meet the interest. They've agreed to accept Sybylla's services as a governess instead.

SYBYLLA: I'm being traded for my father's debts. Mother's decided I must sacrifice myself and be as miserable as her!

HELEN: Think of your brothers and sisters—

SYBYLLA: Why can't I think of myself?

GRANNIE: A woman doesn't think of herself!

SYBYLLA: But what about my career?

GRANNIE: What career? Daydreaming and reading books? Join the real world, Sybylla.

HELEN: [*looking at the letter*] Where is she sending her?

GRANNIE: To the … M'Swats? They have a pig farm at Barney's Gap.

SYBYLLA: They're sending me to hell!

HELEN: It says it's only for two years, Sybylla.

SYBYLLA: TWO YEARS??

HELEN: Oh sorry, three, it says three. Couldn't read the cursive.

SYBYLLA: THREE!

GRANNIE: Well child, what do you say?

SYBYLLA: …

Why do you ask me when I don't have a choice?

Harry? Harry!

You guys—off!

She sends GRANNIE *and* HELEN *away and calls for* HARRY.

Harry! I know! I know now, I've come to tell you—I know everything! Your ring, I want to wear it.

HARRY: Sybylla—

SYBYLLA: We can get married.

>*She holds out her ring finger.*

Where's that ring, cummon, shove it on.

>*She gets down on one knee.*

I do. Look, see? I do. Let's get this show on the road.

HARRY: Sybylla, I can't marry you.

>HARRY *pulls her up.*

SYBYLLA: What? Is there someone else? It's Blanche, isn't it! I knew it! That beautiful minx! Blanche? Where is she?

HARRY: No, Syb, no … I've lost Five Bob. The bank's foreclosed … I've lost everything. I'm sort of relieved, really.

SYBYLLA: **WHAT IS GOING ON?**

HARRY: The drought finally got me. I ought to have told you, but I thought I could fix it. I'll get work somewhere.

SYBYLLA: Take me with you.

HARRY: I couldn't do that to you.

SYBYLLA: **Did I even want to go with him?**

HARRY: I won't let you throw your lot in with a nobody.

SYBYLLA: **Did I just want him to feel better?**

HARRY: Well, I guess this is it.

SYBYLLA: **What did I want??**

>Harry.

>I know what it is to be poor. I could be of use to you. I want to be useful. I'm coming with you.

HARRY: I won't let you do that to yourself.

SYBYLLA: I don't get to choose, huh?

HARRY: I'll fix this for us. And I'll come back for you.

SYBYLLA: …

>Go and grab the world by the horns, Harry. Be the man that you are and show it who's boss.

>*He takes this as a yes. A lil smile creeps on his face, he turns to walk away.*

HARRY: I'll see you, Syb.

>*He holds up his whip to give it a final crack—*

SYBYLLA: You don't have to do that.
HARRY: Okay.

> SYBYLLA *gets on a buggy and horse. Her joyous journey to Caddagat in Act One repeats in a now miserable journey to Barney's Gap. The fiddler and the drummer travel with her.*

SYBYLLA: **There he goes. Riding off into the sunset to take fate into his own hands. Here I am. Riding on a buggy to a pig farm to yell at sticky children.**

> **And all a girl can do? Is choose to make peace … with having no choice at all.**

> **It's okay, I'm a woman in outback Australia, 1897, statistically I could die any minute and the way my story is going, nothing would surprise me.**

> **Goodbye Five Bob.**
> **Goodbye Caddagat.**
> **Goodbye reading, writing, music … personal hygiene.**

> *The* M'SWATS *arrive.*

And hello M'Swats.

> *Song: 'THE WILL (M'SWAT)'.*

FAMILY: [*singing*]
> —M'Swat. M'Swat
> You're not. A M'Swat

JIMMY: [*singing*]
> We know enough to know just what is what

KIDS: [*singing*]
> M'Swat

JIMMY: [*singing*]
> We know how much your old man hasn't got

KIDS: [*singing*]
> M'Swat

JIMMY: [*singing*]
> He loves the piss but he ain't got no pot

KIDS: [*singing*]
> M'Swat

JIMMY: [*singing*]
> And that's a thing we'll make sure ain't forgot

KIDS: [*singing*]
> M'Swat

JIMMY: [*singing*]
> Where there's a will there's a way

KIDS: [*singing*]
> Way!

JIMMY: [*singing*]
> And while you're here it's my way

KIDS: [*singing*]
> Our way!

JIMMY: [*singing*]
> I've got the skill to kill your day

KIDS: [*singing*]
> Hey!

JIMMY: [*singing*]
> So fill out your will or get back on the highway

M'SWAT *and* MRS M *enter. She might be pregnant.*

M'SWAT: The name's M'Swat and that there's the missus. Orright, kids, I'm off for a bit, but this is Miss Melvyn. Don't give her no cheek just cos she's poor Dick Melvyn's daughter. That's Lizer.

SYBYLLA: Morning.

M'SWAT: Rose-Jane.

SYBYLLA: Morning.

M'SWAT: Bullant.

SYBYLLA: Bullant?

BULLANT *pinches her.*

Arch?

LIZER: Bullant pinches.

JIMMY: I'm Jimmy. I'm man of the house while Dad's away.

LIZER: What about Peter?

ROSE-JANE: Wait till she meets Peter …

SYBYLLA: Who is Peter?

M'SWAT: He's me heir. He's almost eighteen.

LIZER: Peter shaves.

M'SWAT: Yeah the Missus 'n' I lost a few between Peter 'n' Lizer.

SYBYLLA: How many have you had?

M'SWAT: Noine maybe ten who knows hahahaha.

MRS M: There's been twelve all up.

SYBYLLA: Twelve!

M'SWAT: Alright I'll see youz in a few months. Don't worry, Missus M
will keep 'em in line, and Peter'll be back in a few weeks.

LIZER: Peter's muscly.

> M'SWAT *exits.*

SYBYLLA: Why don't we start with penmanship?

JIMMY: What?

SYBYLLA: You mean 'I beg your pardon'.

JIMMY: [*singing*]
> The word I said and meant to say was 'what'

KIDS: [*singing*]
> M'Swat

JIMMY: [*singing*]
> And we don't want your fancy-talking rot

KIDS: [*singing*]
> M'Swat

JIMMY: [*singing*]
> You speak like you're some high-bred hoity shot

KIDS: [*singing*]
> M'Swat

JIMMY: [*singing*]
> But we know you got diddly-bloody-squat

KIDS: [*singing*]
> M'Swat

> SYBYLLA *looks at* MRS M *who laughs and raises her eyebrows.*

SYBYLLA: Write down your names, please.

> *They do.* JIMMY *bangs the inkpot.*

Jimmy, please don't bang your inkpot.

> JIMMY *bangs the inkpot.*

Jimmy, please do not bang your inkpot! Now will you please—

JIMMY: I will please myself!

He stands to go. She gets in his way.

FAMILY: [*singing*]
>Where there's a will there's a way

JIMMY: [*singing*]
>And I think we will go fishing

ALL: [*singing*]
>We've had our fill of school today
>So minus yourself, we're out before addition

>JIMMY *heads off and the kids follow.* SYBYLLA *looks at* MRS M *who just laughs.*

MRS M: You'll have your work cut out with them!

>*A week later.* SYBYLLA *paces in front of the kids. She has a small switch behind her back.*

SYBYLLA: This week we will work on the future tense.

JIMMY: What?

SYBYLLA: Beg pardon.

JIMMY: What?

SYBYLLA: Beg pardon!

>*Beat.*

JIMMY: What?

>SYBYLLA *almost pulls switch out, but holds back.*

SYBYLLA: Future tense describes what we're going to do in the future. Miss Melvyn will teach. Jimmy will learn.

JIMMY: [*singing*]
>The future is a bloody lovely spot

KIDS: [*singing*]
>M'Swat

JIMMY: [*singing*]
>For those that have, but not those who have not

KIDS: [*singing*]
>M'Swat

JIMMY: [*singing*]
>And Jimmy will get all that should be got

KIDS: [*singing*]
>   M'Swat
JIMMY: [*singing*]
>   While Miss will get what's in a chamber pot
KIDS: [*singing*]
>   M'Swat
SYBYLLA: Write your name, and what you will do

>   *The other three write but* JIMMY *bangs his inkpot.*

Jimmy, don't bang the inkpot!

>   *He does it louder.*

This is your last warning.

>   JIMMY *bangs the pot real good.* SYBYLLA *brings the switch across his arm. Shocked silence. He yells. They join him. Another small smack.* MRS M *runs in and screams. Breaks switch and grabs* JIMMY *to her.*

MRS M: You little rat girl! Poor boy! She'd have you dead if I didn't come in! No more school today!

>   MRS M *and kids march out,* JIMMY *last.*

JIMMY: [*singing*]
>   Where there's a will, there's a way
>   And I will be winner, missy
>   Poor Melvyn's girl is stuck here, eh?
>   So don't push your luck or I'll actually get pissy

>   *The parlour. Kids slopping around.* MRS M *enters.*

MRS M: Now I know we had a bit of a to-do last week, but this'll cheer you up. Meet the handsomest member of the M'Swat clan.
BULLANT: S'Peter!
ROSE-JANE: S'Peter!
MRS M: It's me eldest, S'Peter!

>   PETER *walks in. A very tall, awkward boy,* SYBYLLA*'s age.*

LIZER: S'Peter's here.
PETER: G'day Lize.

>   *She swoons.*

You're Poor Dick Melvyn's daughter?

SYBYLLA: Ah, the M'Swat heir!

MRS M: I made pie for you, Peter.

LIZER: Peter likes pie.

PETER: Naw I just come in to wash up, I'm out visiting tonight.

FAMILY: —Oooooooh.

LIZER: [*very sad*] Peter's taken.

PETER: I'm round for a bit now. Syb was it? Let me know if ya need anything.

He does a saucy wink and leaves. LIZER *glares at her.*

MRS M: Here we go! All the girls fall for Peter.

The school room. The students. SYBYLLA *paces.*

SYBYLLA: This week we will master the future tense. Show me what you've written.

ROSE-JANE: [*singing*]
　　　Rose-Jane will learn to not pee in her cot

BULLANT: [*singing*]
　　　Bullant will get real good at the sling shot

LIZER: [*singing*]
　　　And Lizer will use hankies for her snot

SYBYLLA: And Jimmy? What will you do?

Pause. JIMMY *bangs the inkpot.*

Alright. I'll tell you what Jimmy will do:
　[*Singing*]
　　　He will not ever bang that damned inkpot

SYBYLLA *smacks him across the shoulders with the switch. He yells. The others join. She smacks it across the desk, silencing them all.*

JIMMY *screams.* MRS M *comes screaming in from the next room.* SYBYLLA *raises the rod and stares at her. She shuts up.* JIMMY *stops, surprised.*

You're just in time to see an educational breakthrough, Mrs M'Swat. These children will learn the only thing they ever need to learn: that life is hard and hope is useless. There's no point learning about future tense, because I'm tellin' ya kids, this misery IS MY FUTURE!

[*Singing*]
      Where there's a will there's a way
Bang!
      And while I'm here it's my way
Bang!
      I've got the skill to seize the day
Breaks stick.
      So fill up your quill and hit the learning highway
The kids and MRS M *join one by one, suddenly a polished choir.*

[*Singing*]
      And
And BULLANT: [*singing*]
      That
And ROSE-JANE: [*singing*]
      Is
And LIZER: [*singing*]
      What
And JIMMY: [*singing*]
      Is
And MRS M: [*singing*]
      What!
ALL: [*singing*]
      M'Swat!

      The M'SWATS *scatter about.*

      Months later. SYBYLLA *sits at the tumbledown piano, striking a repetitive off key note.*

LIZER: Sybyyyyllllla you have a letter?

      SYBYLLA *doesn't look up.*

SYBYLLA: Is it fateful?
LIZER: Ummmmm.
SYBYLLA: Who's it from.
LIZER: Your mum.
SYBYLLA: Practise your reading. Go on.

LIZER: 'Sybylla. You've barely served half a year as governess, stop writing me begging to return to Caddagat, it is not possible, as I have sent Gertie there in your stead—'

SYBYLLA: Yep, it's fateful.

LIZER: 'What is wrong with the M'Swats—Is it too much work?'

SYBYLLA: No.

LIZER: 'Are they unkind to you?'

SYBYLLA: No.

LIZER: 'They cannot possibly be the gar … gar—'

SYBYLLA: Gargoyles.

LIZER: ' … you describe …

> LIZER *squints suspiciously at* SYBYLLA, *a là Uma Thurman in* Kill Bill.

… I have always been a good mother to you—'

SYBYLLA: No.

LIZER: 'Two more years is the least you can do in return. Life is not always about pleasure.'

> SYBYLLA *snatches the letter and tears it up into little pieces.*

SYBYLLA: That's right, Lizer. It's about suffocating. It's about disappearing into pointlessness.

> *She returns to the piano.*

> *Song: 'IN THE WRONG KEY' (reprise).*

[*Singing*]
> Will always be stuck right here
> This piano
> May as well be a shelf
> This piano

> SYBYLLA *breaks off as she notices a man watching.*

Harry … !!?

PETER: Nah. S'Peter.

> *Awkward beat … did he hear her?*

SYBYLLA: Sorry, I thought you were … someone I used to know …

PETER: You think your better than us, don't ya.

SYBYLLA: No. I think all humans are equal and deserve respect—

PETER: Nah you don't. '*Gargoyles*'? I seen you look at us. You think we're a bunch of grots. But you miss the jokes and fun we have. You look like you sucked a lemon half the time. But our family's together and yours sent you away. We got money from being smart, and we lend it to stuck-up families like yours. So don't try your airs on us.

SYBYLLA: You're right, I'm not better.

PETER: It's an honest life. We're happy with wot God gave us, and you should be too—you're alive, aren't ya?

> PETER *leaves.* SYBYLLA *uses the piano to work out where she's at.*
>
> *Song: 'GARGOYLE'.*

SYBYLLA: [*singing*]
>> Am I alive?
>> I feel like stone
>> Judging from above
>> A gargoyle
>> I'm the gargoyle
>>
>> Am I so wise?
>> Maybe I'm blind
>> Seeing without love
>> A gargoyle
>> I'm the gargoyle
>>
>> Screaming to be heard, not to hear
>> Wanting to be seen, not to see
>> Is the world around what I fear
>> Or is it me?
>> The lack in me?
>>
>> Am I alone?
>> Or just asleep?
>> Can I break the spell
>> On the gargoyle?
>>
>> Am I unique?
>> Or more like you?

> Is there more to tell
> Than I knew as the gargoyle?
> I don't have to be the gargoyle

LIZER *has crept in.*

LIZER: What's that?

SYBYLLA: It's something I wrote.

LIZER: You can write music?

SYBYLLA: Yes. I can.

LIZER: I can't do that.

SYBYLLA: If you want to, you can. Here, I'll show you.

> SYBYLLA *shows her some notes to play, that harmonise.* LIZER
> *swoons.* ROSE-JANE *soon comes in.*

ROSE-JANE: I want to play too.

SYBYLLA: Come on then.

> MRS M *and the rest enter and join.*

MRS M: Peter! They're having a recital! Lizer's playin' the peanny!!

PETER: S'bloody great, Syb.

SYBYLLA: S'Peter, here, you play this with Lizer—

The whole family play together.

[*Singing*]

> Let the sunlight warm, it won't burn
> Let yourself be here, you can stay
> And teach yourself, instead, to learn
> And to play
> To play

ALL: [*singing*]

> So play with me, play with me, play with me-e-e-e-e
> So play with me, play with me, play with me-e-e-e-e
> So play with me, play with me, play with me-e-e-e-e
> Play with me

> M'SWAT *has entered, watching his family dancing around, real*
> *cultured. He clocks* PETER *fiddling around at the keys, smiling at*
> SYBYLLA, *who smiles back.*

M'SWAT: How's my zoo going?

PETER: Ms Sybylla's teaching us how to play, Dad. It's really s'pretty.

SYBYLLA: S'Peter is a great … S'Pupil, Mr M'Swat! We'll have him at the Theatre Royal in no time!

He looks at his wife. Uh-oh.

M'SWAT: Ah will ya now? That's wonderful. Ah, Ms Melvyn, can I bend your ear for a second?

SYBYLLA *joins him.*

M'SWAT: Miss Melvyn, you been right good to our kids. But I know what's going' on here. Our S'Peter's gone and cast his spell on you. But you can't marry him. He's good as made it with Susie Duffy, and her ole da has some property I want our s'Pete to have, and I wouldn't want ya to spoil the fun. But don't worry. Susie's got a brother, and I could have a word with Old Duffy for a hook-up.

MRS M: His son's not made like our S'Peter but—

SYBYLLA: Oh no, you've misunderstood. / I'm just teaching him—

MRS M: It's alright girl. / We're sending you back to Possum Gully.

SYBYLLA: Whoa whoa whoa what?

MRS M: You gotta get over him love.

SYBYLLA *stares at her, then throws herself into her arms crying.*

SYBYLLA: Oh, oh, oh, wha thank you! S'true. So embarrassing but soon as I saw S'Peter I was like, 'whoa S'Peter's such a s'punk'—

The family return, sans JIMMY.

M'SWAT: 'N' tell your father he needn't worry about the money. You've done us well.

SYBYLLA: Oh. You are very kind people.

MRS M: Yeah we are.

M'SWAT: What's the good of being alive if you can't help each other.

LIZER: Will you write me?

SYBYLLA: Yes, Lizer, yes! Honour bright.

LIZER: What?

SYBYLLA: Don't worry.

LIZER: [*to* PETER] I can write letters now.

PETER: You're a ripper, Lize.

LIZER *swoons.*

I'll take you to the station, Syb.

M'SWAT: Nope nope no need, no need! I'm heading out that way anyway. I'll take her.

SYBYLLA: I'll grab my bag.

> JIMMY *comes in with her baggage and keeps walking with them, he speaks in a recitative tone.*

JIMMY: 'Jimmy will take your bags.' 'Jimmy has mastered the future tense.'

ALL: [*singing*]
> AND THAT IS WHAT IS WHAT
> M'SWAT!

> SYBYLLA *returns to Possum Gully.* MRS M *transforms into* LUCY *while the rest rejoin the* BALLADEERS.

SYBYLLA: **Possum Gully. I, Sybylla Melvyn, am back where I started. Almost grateful to stand in the scorching furnace wind.**

LUCY: Even the pig farmer wanted a refund on you.

> SYBYLLA *sees* LUCY*'s round belly.*

SYBYLLA: **My mother! What a relief to see her ladylike face.**
Are you having a baby?

LUCY: What does it look like?

SYBYLLA: **Poor Lucy. She nearly had a minute to herself, but the cycle of motherhood began again.**

DICK: Hey there, Prince.

SYBYLLA: **My father. An honest man who once had big dreams but surrendered to drink when the debts piled up.**

DICK: Back to pick a fight, are ya? They treat you alright?

SYBYLLA: It's fine, Dad, they looked after me.

DICK: Orright, Prince.

HORACE: I'm off, Syb.

SYBYLLA: **My little brother.**

HORACE: Dad's a useless bastard. Not gonna waste my life while he pisses his away. I'm gonna go make a name for myself.

SYBYLLA: **All grown up with dreams of his own—**

> LUCY *hugs* HORACE. SYBYLLA *notices the pain in her mother's eyes as she breaks hug.*

It hurts her to say goodbye to her children. I never noticed.

LUCY: Horace and Gertie gone. Ah, it's for the best.

> DICK *exits.*

SYBYLLA: **In her whole life, my mother had only ever been told—
'obey thy husband'. But was she cursed with my fever for
something more? My fever for the unattainable? Is it burning
inside her somewhere?**

LUCY: Sybylla …

> *She goes to share with* SYBYLLA. *But changes her mind.*

Come. There's work to do.

> LUCY *exits.*

SYBYLLA: **Maybe not, but what is in her, is a grit that is far beyond
my comprehension. A bravery to stand in all this … littleness.
This everyday littleness.**

> **I'm a goddamn coward.**

> **And then, OF COURSE, the fateful letters started to arrive:**

> *Song: 'WORKING MY WAY'.*

HARRY: Dearest Syb—

> [*Singing*]

> I know you told me not to write
> So I'm prepared for another fight
> You always find a way to cut me through
> But since we split I've crossed the land
> And learned how much a man can stand
> When one day he'll be standing next to you

> I worked until my legs gave out
> I worked until I fried
> I worked because I had no doubt
> I was working my way back to your side

> I took a thousand cattle west
> A coupla months and not a lotta rest
> But got a hefty sum for pushing through
> And then I hit the cane up top
> And hacked and hacked without a stop
> I'll stop when there's a priest before us two

I worked until my arms gave out
I worked until I fried
I worked because I had no doubt
I was working my way back to your side

I thought it was my birthright
That I deserved my life
I only want to earn it back
To earn myself a wife

And so I took the chance and wrote
So hear me out and don't cut my throat
For fortune's come my way again, it's true!
Some distant cousin left a will
And left me, Syb, a bloody mil!
I've bought Five Bob for me, and yes, for you

I worked until my luck came back
I worked and worked with pride
I worked and now I have no doubt
I was working my way back to your side
So let's not wait till twenty-one
There's nothing left to hide
I worked to win the only one
That I want working back by my side

'Can you believe it, Syb! I fixed it! When things are settled in a few months, I'm coming to claim you. I've seen Gertie a good many times, she's not a bit like you— Love, your punching-bag, Harry.'

SYBYLLA: **Claim me, will you?**

HARRY *disappears. She opens the next letter.*

Oh!! And my Gertie?

GERTIE, *three years older and blooming into her adult self, appears and speaks her letter.*

GERTIE: 'Dearest Sybylla, Caddagat is lovely—Harold Beecham insists I call him Harry, he took me to Five Bob last week, and it was lovely fun. We went on a boat and everything!'

SYBYLLA: **That friggin boat.**

She opens the next letter.

GERTIE: 'Dearest Sybylla, Harry says I am the prettiest little girl that ever was, and he gave me such a lovely bracelet. I wish you could see it.'

SYBYLLA: **Braaaaacelet? Orrkaaaaaayyyyyyy.**

She opens the next letter.

GERTIE: 'Dearest Sybylla, there is to be a ball next month, Harry says I am to keep all my dances for him … ' We've spent nearly every day together this last month—'

SYBYLLA: Oh, I see …

GERTIE *swirls off as* LUCY *re-enters.*

LUCY: Any news?

SYBYLLA: Yes. Good news. Very good news. The right news.

LUCY: Did you meet Harold Beecham at Caddagat? Grannie says he's spending a lot of time with Gertie. That would be useful, he's immensely rich again, apparently. He's been asking the best route to Possum Gully. He must be coming to ask for Gertie's hand.

SYBYLLA: If he puts a gun to his head, he'll get to Possum Gully soon enough.

LUCY *laughs, unexpectedly. Two weary women looking at each other. She collects herself.*

LUCY: You're very wicked, Sybylla. The doilies need ironing.

SYBYLLA *burst into tears and pulls her apron over her head.* LUCY *pays more attention than usual.*

Don't cry on them or you'll have to wash them again.

LUCY *exits.*

SYBYLLA: **Pretty Gertie. Handsome Harry. Silly Sybylla. Now there's a story that makes sense: The hero inherits a fortune then finds true love with the right woman. Troll goes back to farm.**

To whom am I now necessary? Will a noisy girl ever be necessary?

I remained at Possum Gully to tread the same old life in its tame narrow path, until my ninenteenth birthday, a day only distinguished from the three hundred and sixty-four other crappy days of the year … by cake.

HARRY: [*Irish*] Forgive me madam, could you tell me the way to Possum Gully?

SYBYLLA: Go away! How did you find me?

HARRY: Your mother said you'd be in the paddocks muttering to yourself. Let me help you—

He helps her up, they stare at each other, not knowing what is between them.

SYBYLLA: I don't want you to see me like this.

HARRY: You haven't replied to any of my letters.

SYBYLLA: Go on, just … do it. Say it. Get it over with.

HARRY: You know what I'm going to say.

SYBYLLA: Yes, say it all, I promise I won't be nasty. I was right, you were wrong, you could never love a perverse girl like me, you've found a better model, that's Gertie, and that's okay.

HARRY: Gertie?

SYBYLLA: And yes, of course I will keep our engagement quiet. No-one need know we were so daft.

HARRY: Gertie!! You thought—I've never thought of her in any way but as *our* little sister.

SYBYLLA: What?

HARRY: I've been looking after her like a brother. I want you, Syb.

SYBYLLA: No, no, no Gertie is good, twenty times as good as me, and pretty—

HARRY: Pretty is nothing, anyone can be pretty. But you are … you! No-one is like you.

SYBYLLA: Okay, well, I LOVE that.
Harry I—

HARRY: I want to give you everything, Syb. But you're the queerest girl, I can't work out what it is you want.

He pulls him close to her, SYBYLLA *resists momentarily then submits to his arms.*

SYBYLLA: Oh Harry! I don't know either … I just can't.
I have a fever. A fever to make something of myself.
I want to write.
I want to be a writer.

HARRY: A writer? Is that all!? You can have your own study, I'll work all day, you can write your … stuff, help me with my letters. My wife, the writer! It'll be perfect, Syb.

HARRY laughs and scoops her into an embrace.

We are going to be so great!

SYBYLLA: Oh, Harry, I can't.

HARRY: What's the matter? What are you so worried about?

SYBYLLA: I'll be Sybylla the wife. Then Sybylla the mother. Then maybe I'll die, giving birth to your child. When will I ever have been Sybylla the writer?

HARRY: But you'll be mine.

SYBYLLA: Exactly.

The party. We might see LUCY, DICK *and* HARRY *with a lit birthday cake?*

Why write? Why does anyone write? Men write, and they know they will be heard. I'd like to be heard. To voice the things around me. I see things as they are, that is my gift, but my God … I think it is my curse.

We'll all die and become a pile of nothing crumbs in this dirt, so what will it matter if I have been silly or smart. Great or small. Loud or quiet. So long as I have been true? So long as I have tried?

Gah. Being nineteen is exhausting.

SYBYLLA blows out the candles. The next day.

HARRY: How did you sleep?

SYBYLLA: Awful. You?

HARRY: Awful. Like I used to before Christmas. Awake all night hoping the Aunts had figured out what I really wanted.

SYBYLLA: What did you want?

HARRY: Everything a little boy wants, I spose.

SYBYLLA: Me too, I'm afraid.

HARRY: Oh.

SYBYLLA: Yesterday I told you I wanted to be a writer. I wrote this for you.

She reads her letter.

Dearest Harry,

[*Singing*]
> You get me feeling stuck-stuck-stuck in the air
> Cos you try to, try to take away every care
> But if you—as you—smooth away my fate
> You smooth away the bit of me that's worth something, mate
> And so I write to let you know
> I love you and you have to go
> I need to find myself what waits in store
> We're mates …
> Mates and nothing more

With great affection, your friend, Sybylla.

She folds the letter and passes it to him.

HARRY: What are you going to write?

SYBYLLA: Oooh I don't know … a fictitious memoir? It will never work.

HARRY: Send me a copy.

He touches her cheek one last time.

SYBYLLA: **And Harold Beecham tipped his hat … and was gone.**

> HARRY *returns to the* BALLADEERS. *And* SYBYLLA *feels terribly alone. She sits at the piano, determined, focussed, writing.* LUCY *enters, trying to hide her distress.*

[*Skimming through her work fast and, lightly, under her breath*] 'This is my first recollection of life, I was barely three.'

LUCY: Sybylla, have you chopped the firewood?

SYBYLLA: 'I can remember the majestic gum trees surrounding us.'

LUCY: Sybylla, I know you're ignoring me!

SYBYLLA: 'I sobbed big fat tears then Father said, "Daddy's little mate isn't gonna cry like a girl, is she?"'

LUCY: You're a careless washer, you've put your father's trousers on the boil and the colour's run out of them—

SYBYLLA: 'I could ride among the musterers as gamely as any of the big sunburnt bushmen.'

LUCY: SYBYLLA!

SYBYLLA: [*firmly*] Mother. I cannot care about Father's trousers. I have done my chores and now I am writing. This is my time. Please.

>*Beat.*

LUCY: Mr Beecham left. He didn't ask for Gertie. He was our last hope—

SYBYLLA: No he isn't, Mother.

LUCY: I have failed this family.

SYBYLLA: No you didn't. You did what you thought you should. And that's all we can do. Sit down.

>LUCY *does.*

You work too hard, Mum. Come on, play with me.

>SYBYLLA *starts 'Play With Me' theme in left and* LUCY *does excellent right hand.*

SYBYLLA: You're good!

LUCY: Of course I am. I'm good at everything.

>Hurry up and finish your book.

>*She exits,* SYBYLLA *swings into her favourite position at her piano.*

SYBYLLA: **My dear fellow Australians. This story is all about me. No, about all the things that forged me. If it is any good, I do not know, it may very well sound like a couple of nails in a rusty tin pot.**

>**Time rules us all, and life, indeed, does not go how we plan it, and we women cannot choose our lot ... but it's 1899 goddammit, can't we choose a little bit? Can't we choose to write a little bit here, and a little bit there, wake up before the cows and put down a yarn ... yes, I lack experience but ...**

>*Song: 'SOMEONE LIKE ME'.*

[*Singing*]
>>If I say what I think
>>If I say what I see
>>I might reach
>>Someone like me

If I say what I feel
And demand what I'll be
I might reach
Someone like me

If I look in the mirror
And truly see it
It's not so scary to be it
If I put it on paper
And truly say it
I'll be it
I can play it

If I write with some care
Of the world that I see
Then I'm free …
And I might free someone like me

ALL: [*singing*]

Someone like me
Someone like me
Someone like me
Someone like me
If I say what I think
If I say what I see
I might reach
Someone like me
If I say what I feel
And demand what I'll be
I might reach
Someone like me

If I look in the mirror
And truly see it
It's not so scary to be it
If I put it on paper
And truly say it
I'll be it

SYBYLLA: [*singing*]

I can play it …

Sybylla, you know nothing. But you know what it is to be a girl who wants everything under this blazing southern sky.

She reads her work out loud to us for the first time.

'The great sun is sinking in the west, grinning and winking as he goes, upon the starving stock and drought-smitten wastes of land. Nearer he draws to the gum-tree scrubby horizon, turning the clouds to orange, scarlet, silver-flame, gold! The kookaburras laugh their merry mocking good-night; the stars peep shyly out.

To my sisters, my brothers—all us children on this sunburned soil. I love you. I love you. I'm proud to be you.'

Gosh, this is sentimental.

Don't skip it.

[*Singing*]

     If I write with some care of the girl—

     The woman I see

     Then I'm free

     And I might free someone like me

SYBYLLA *continues to write. The sun finally goddamn sets.* ~~AMEN.~~ *AWOMEN.*

THE END

NEXTSTAGE

Developed by Monash University, Melbourne, as part of the Jeanne Pratt Artist in Residency program, which culminated in a developmental staging directed by Petra Kalive with dramaturgy by Anna Barnes. Further development funded by City of Stonnington and Melbourne Theatre Company's NEXT STAGE Writers' Program.

With a $4.6 million investment by Melbourne Theatre Company and Melbourne Theatre Company's Playwrights Giving Circle, the NEXT STAGE Writers' Program has introduced the most rigorous playwright commissioning and development process ever undertaken by the Company, setting a new benchmark for play development in Australia.

Thank you for sharing our passion and commitment to Australian stories and Australian writers.

PLAYWRIGHTS GIVING CIRCLE

Thank you to Melbourne Theatre Company's Playwrights Giving Circle – its donors, foundations and organisations – for sharing our passion and commitment to Australian stories and Australian writers.

Tony & Janine Burgess, Fitzpatrick Sykes Family Foundation, Jane Hansen AO & Paul Little AO, Larry Kamener & Petra Kamener, Susanna Mason & Ken MacMahon, Helen Nicolay, Pimlico Foundation, Tania Seary & Chris Lynch, Craig Semple, Dr Richard Simmie, Derek Young AM & Caroline Young

MALCOLM ROBERTSON FOUNDATION

The Vizard FOUNDATION

Melbourne Theatre Company

Our Donors

We gratefully acknowledge the ongoing support of our leading Donors.

LIFETIME PATRONS

Acknowledging a lifetime of extraordinary support.

Rowland Ball OAM &
   The Late Monica Maughan
Pat Burke
Peter Clemenger AO &
   The Late Joan Clemenger AO
Greig Gailey &
   Dr Geraldine Lazarus

Allan Myers AC KC &
   Maria Myers AC
The Late Biddy Ponsford
The Late Dr Roger Riordan AM
Maureen Wheeler AO &
   Tony Wheeler AO

The Late Ursula Whiteside
Caroline Young &
   Derek Young AM

ENDOWMENT FUND DONORS

Supporting Melbourne Theatre Company's long-term sustainability and creative future.

Leading Gifts

Jane Hansen AO & Paul Little AO
The Late Max Schultz &
   The Late Jill Schultz
The University of Melbourne

$50,000+

The Late Margaret Anne Brien
Tony & Janine Burgess
John Higgins AO &
   Jodie Maunder
Martin & Loreto Hosking
The Late Valerie Gwendolyn King
The Late Biddy Ponsford
Tania Seary & Chris Lynch
The John & Myriam Wylie
   Foundation

$20,000+

Andrew Sisson AO &
   Tracey Sisson
Prudence & Neil Morrison

$10,000+

Helen Lynch AM & Helen Bauer
Jennifer Darbyshire &
   David Walker
Ian Hicks AO
Tony & Nathalie Johnson
Jane Kunstler
Craig Semple

PLAYWRIGHTS GIVING CIRCLE

Supporting the NEXT STAGE Writers' Program, our industry-leading commissioning initiative.

Tony & Janine Burgess, Fitzpatrick Sykes Family Foundation, Jane Hansen AO & Paul Little AO,
Larry Kamener & Petra Kamener, Susanna Mason & Ken MacMahon, Helen Nicolay, Pimlico Foundation,
Tania Seary & Chris Lynch, Craig Semple, Dr Richard Simmie, Derek Young AM & Caroline Young

MALCOLM ROBERTSON FOUNDATION

The Vizard FOUNDATION

TRUSTS & FOUNDATIONS

Cybec Foundation

The Gailey Lazarus Foundation

HANSEN LITTLE FOUNDATION

The Ian Potter Foundation

THE ROBERT SALZER FOUNDATION

telematics trust

trawalla foundation

NEWSBOYS FOUNDATION

JOHN & MYRIAM Wylie

VICTORIA State Government

Annual giving

Acknowledging Donors whose recent gifts help enrich and transform lives through the magic of theatre.

Current as of September 2024.

BENEFACTORS CIRCLE

$50,000+

Tony & Janine Burgess
Krystyna Campbell-Pretty AM
Peter Clemenger AO
Jane Hansen AO & Paul Little AO
John Higgins AO & Jodie Maunder
Martin & Loreto Hosking

The Late Valerie Gwendolyn King
The Late Max &
  the Late Jill Schultz
Tania Seary & Chris Lynch
Andrew Sisson AO &
  Tracey Sisson

Fitzpatrick Sykes Family
  Foundation
Maureen Wheeler AO &
  Tony Wheeler AO
The John & Myriam Wylie
  Foundation

$20,000+

Joanna Baevski
Edith Burgess
Linda Herd

The Margaret Lawrence Bequest
Ian & Margaret McKellar
Prudence & Neil Morrison

Craig Semple

$10,000+

Alan & Mary-Louise Archibald
  Foundation
John & Lorraine Bates
Helen Lynch AM & Helen Bauer
Jay Bethell & Peter Smart
Michael Buxton AM &
  Janet Buxton
Kathleen Canfell
Angie & Colin Carter
The Cattermole Family
Jennifer Darbyshire &
  David Walker
The Dowd Foundation

Charles & Cornelia Goode
  Foundation
John & Joan Grigg OAM
Ian Hicks AO
Diane John
Tony & Nathalie Johnson
Petra & Larry Kamener
Daryl Kendrick &
  Leong Lai Peng (Betty)
Suzanne Kirkham
Susanna Mason
Helen Nicolay
Pimlico Foundation

Catherine Quealy
Janet Reid OAM & Allan Reid
Lisa Ring
Anne & Mark Robertson OAM
Dr Richard Simmie
Rob Stewart & Lisa Dowd
Tintagel Bay P/L
Ralph Ward-Ambler AM &
  Barbara Ward-Ambler
Matt Williams – Artem Group
Anonymous (2)

$5,000+

Bagôt Gjergja Foundation
James Best & Doris Young
Paul & Wendy Bonnici & Family
Bowness Family Foundation
Dr Douglas Brown &
  Treena Brown
Dr Andrew Buchanan &
  Peter Darcy
Ian & Jillian Buchanan
Bill Burdett AM & Sandra Burdett
Pat Burke & Jan Nolan
Diana Burleigh
Alison & John Cameron
Ann Cutts
Prof Glyn Davis AC &
  Prof Margaret Gardner AC

Melody & Jonathan Feder
Christine Gilbertson
Roger & Jan Goldsmith
Lesley Griffin
David & Lily Harris
Jane Hemstritch AO
Tony Hillery &
  Warwick Eddington
Bruce & Mary Humphries
Sam & Jacky Hupert
Dr Sonay Hussein, in memory
  of Prof David Penington AC
Karen Inge & Dr George Janko
Amy & Paul Jasper
Josephine & Graham Kraehe AO
Jane Kunstler

Martin & Melissa McIntosh
Kim & Peter Monk
George & Rosa Morstyn
The Myer Foundation
Tom & Ruth O'Dea
Leigh O'Neill
Roger & Ruth Parker
Dr Kia Pajouhesh
  (Smile Solutions)
Renzella Family
Lynne Sherwood
Geoffrey Smith & Gary Singer
Trawalla Foundation Trust
Janet Whiting AM & Phil Lukies
Rebecca Wilkinson
Anonymous (8)

ADVOCATES CIRCLE

$2,500+

Ros Boyce
Paul & Robyn Brasher
Nigel & Sheena Broughton
Geoff Cosgriff
Susanne Dahn
Ann Darby
Megan Davis & Antony Isaacson
The Dodge Family Foundation
Rodney Dux
Anna & John Field
Nigel & Cathy Garrard
Diana & Murray Gerstman
Charlies Gillies & Penny Allen
Heather & Bob Glindemann OAM
Henry Gold

Charles & Cornelia
   Goode Foundation
Jane Grover
Halina Lewenberg Charitable
   Foundation
Peter & Halina Jacobsen
Leg Up Foundation
Professor Duncan Maskell &
   Dr Sarah Maskell
Margaret & John Mason OAM
Don & Sue Matthews
Sandra Murdoch
Jane & Andrew Murray
The Myer Foundation
Nelson Bros Funeral Services
The Orloff Family Charitable Trust

Jeremy Ruskin & Roz Zalewski
In memory of Marysia &
   Berek Segan AM OBE
Brian Snape AM &
   Christina Martin
Geoff Steinicke
Ricci Swart AM
James & Anne Syme
Richard & Debra Tegoni
Liz Tromans
The Veith Foundation
Price & Christine Williams
The Ray & Margaret Wilson
   Foundation
Gillian & Tony Wood
Anonymous (3)

LOYALTY CIRCLE

$1,000+

Prof Noel Alpins AM & Sylvia Alpins
Margaret Astbury
Ian Baker & Cheryl Saunders
Prof Robin Batterham
Sandra Beanham
Angelina Beninati
Judy Bourke
Steve & Terry Bracks AM
David Reckenberg & Dale Bradbury
Jenny & Lucinda Brash
Bernadette Broberg
Beth Brown &
   The Late Tom Bruce AM
Nan Brown
Rob & Sal Bruce
Julie Burke
Katie Burke
Geoffrey Bush & Michael Riordan
Pam Caldwell
Helen & Dugald Campbell
John & Jan Campbell
Jessica Canning
Clare Carlson
Chernov Family
Assoc Prof Lyn Clearihan &
   Dr Anthony Palmer
Sandy & Yvonne Constantine
Barry & Deborah Conyngham
Karen Cusack
Sue & John Denmead
Mark Duckworth PSM &
   Lauren Mosso
Dr Sally Duguid & Dr David Tingay
Pam Durrant
Jan & Rob Flew
Bev & Geoff Edwards
Karen & David Elias
Anne Evans & Graham Evans AO
Marian Evans

Dr Alastair Fearn
Peter Fearnside & Roxane Hislop
Paul & Mary Fildes
Grant Fisher & Helen Bird
Rosemary Forbes & Ian Hocking
Bruce Freeman
Gaye & John Gaylard
Fiona Griffiths & Tony Osmond
Gill Family Foundation
Ian & Wendy Haines
Charles Harkin
M D Harper
Mark & Jennifer Hayes
Luke Heagerty
Lorraine Hendrata
Brett & Kerri Hereward
Dr Alice Hill & Mark Nicholson
Emeritus Prof Andrea Hull AO
Nanette Hunter
Ann & Tony Hyams AM
Peter Jaffe & Judy Gold
Neil Jens
Ben Johnson & Mark McNamara
Sally & Rod Johnstone
Lesley & Ian Jones
Leah Kaplan & Barry Levy
Irene Kearsey & Michael Ridley
Malcolm Kemp
Daniel Kilby
Michael Kingston
Fiona Kirwan-Hamilton &
   Brett Parkin
Doris & Steve Klein
Marianne & Arthur Klepfisz
Larry Kornhauser & Natalya Gill
Dr Emma Jane Ladakis
Verona Lea
Alison Leslie
Xue Snowe Li

Peter & Judy Loney
Lord Family
Lording Family Foundation
Kerryn Lowe & Raphael Arndt
Ken & Jan Mackinnon
Karin MacNab
Natasha & Laurence Mandie
Chris Maple
Ian & Judi Marshman
Lesley Mason
Penelope McEniry
Heather & Simon McKeon
Garry McLean
Libby McMeekin
Emeritus Prof Peter McPhee AM
Rosemary Meagher &
   The Late Douglas Meagher
Fiona Menzies
Robert & Helena Mestrovic
Ann Miller AM
Ross & Judy Milne-Pott
MK Futures
Barbara & David Mushin
Sarah Nguyen
Nick Nichola & Ingrid Moyle
Dr Paul Nisselle AM & Sue Nisselle
Sally Noonan
David & Lisa Oertle
Dr Jane & Alan Oppenheim
In loving memory of Richard Park
Dr Annamarie Perlesz
Dare & Andrea Power
Peter Philpott & Robert Ratcliffe
Philip & Gayle Raftery
Sally Redlich
Victoria Redwood
John & Veronica Rickard
Phillip Riggio
Ken & Gail Roche

Roslyn & Richard Rogers Family
S & S Rogerson
B & J Rollason
Sue Rose
Nick & Rowena Rudge
Jenny Russo
Edwina Sahhar
Margaret Sahhar AM
Sandi Foundation
  dedicated to Alec
Alex & Brady Scanlon Giving Fund
Sally & Tim Scott
Jacky & Rupert Sherwood
Diane Silk

Dr John Sime
Pauline & Tony Simioni
Jan Simon
Jane Simon & Peter Cox
Tim & Angela Smith
Annette Smorgon
Dr Ross & Helen Stillwell
Rosemary Stipanov
The Stobart Strauss Foundation
Irene & John Sutton
Rodney & Aviva Taft
Charles Tegner
Frank & Mirium Tisher
John & Anna van Weel

Graham Wademan &
  Michael Bowden
Walter & Gertie Wagner
Kevin & Elizabeth Walsh
Pinky Watson
Kaye & John de Wijn
Ann & Alan Wilkinson
Robert & Diana Wilson
Ralph Wollner &
  The Hon Kirsty Macmillan SC
Mandy & Edward Yencken
Anonymous (27)

EDUCATION GIVING CIRCLE

Acknowledging supporters who are transforming the lives of young Victorians through theatre.

Alan & Mary-Louise
  Archibald Foundation
Joanna Baevski
Judy Bourke
Deborah Conyngham
Geoff Cosgriff
Ann Darby
Grant Fisher & Helen Bird
Bruce Freeman
Mark & Jennifer Hayes

Linda Herd
Neil Jens
Larry Kornhauser OAM &
  Natalya Gill
The Leg Up Foundation
The Myer Foundation
Tom & Ruth O'Dea
John & Veronica Rickard
Anne & Mark Robertson OAM
Ken & Gail Roche

Roslyn & Richard Rogers Family
Andrew Sisson AO &
  Tracey Sisson
Rob Stewart & Lisa Dowd
Richard & Debra Tegoni
Walter & Gertie Wagner
Ann & Alan Wilkinson
Anonymous (4)

LEGACY CIRCLE

Acknowledging supporters who have made the visionary gesture of including
a gift to Melbourne Theatre Company in their will.

John & Lorraine Bates
Mark & Tamara Boldiston
Bernadette Broberg
Adam & Donna Cusack-Muller
Anne Evans & Graham Evans AO
Bruce Freeman
Peter & Betty Game
Edith Gordon

Fiona Griffiths
Linda Herd
Tony Hillery & Warwick Eddington
Jane Kunstler
Irene Kearsey
Robyn & Maurice Lichter
Dr Andrew McAliece &
  Dr Richard Simmie

Libby McMeekin
Peter Philpott & Robert Ratcliffe
Marcus Pettinato
Jillian Smith
Diane Tweeddale
Francis Vergona
Anonymous (16)

Thank you

Melbourne Theatre Company would like to thank the following organisations for their generous support.

Major Partner

Future Directors Initiative Partner

MinterEllison.

Major Marketing Partner

The Monthly
The Saturday Paper
7am

Associate Partners

Challis & Company
Tomorrow's leaders today

Frontier
software
Human Capital Management
& Payroll Software/Services

K&L GATES

THE LANGHAM
MELBOURNE

Supporting Partners

COMMUNE
WINE

Genovese

THE
LUXURY
NETWORK®

invicium

METROPOLIS
EVENTS

QUEST
SOUTHBANK

southgate

Wilson Parking

Marketing Partners

CINEMA
NOVA

RRR

Southbank Theatre Partners

EMPEROR
AUSTRALIA'S HOME OF CHAMPAGNE

mgc
THE
MELBOURNE
GIN COMPANY

SCOTCHMANS HILL
BELLARINE PENINSULA
VICTORIA
ESTABLISHED 1982

www.ingramcontent.com/pod-product-compliance
Lightning Source LLC
Chambersburg PA
CBHW040055100426
42734CB00044B/3320